Donated to
Augustana
University College
by
Augustana's
Students' Union
Capital Development Fund
2001-2004

CANADIAN SPORT TOURISM: AN INTRODUCTION

Wayne Pealo
and
Gerald Redmond

©

Wayne Pealo, Ph.D.
and
Gerald Redmond, Ph.D.

ISBN# 1-896886-04-3

Publisher

Recreation and Tourism Management
Research Institute
Malaspina University College
900 Fifth Street, Nanaimo, B.C.
V9R 5S5

Printed by
Cowichan Press
Unit 3, 3345 Trans-Canada Highway,
Cobble Hill, B.C.
V0R 1L0

2003

ACKNOWLEDGEMENTS

The authors wish to acknowledge the Recreation and Tourism Research Insistute and Malaspina University College for their support with the production of the book. Special recognition goes to Dr. Stu Petersen and the Canadian Congress on Leisure Research for their photographs.

Wayne Pealo
Gerald Redmond

CANADIAN SPORT TOURISM: AN INTRODUCTION

List of Chapters

Introduction: Canadian Sport and Tourism Development in the Twenty-First Century

Sport and Tourism Development in Canada: An Overview

INTRODUCTION: CANADIAN SPORT TOURISM IN THE TWENTY FIRST CENTURY

One of the most succinct definitions of tourism was given in a 1988 American publication (Ellis and Norton, 1988) entitled: *Commercial Recreation*, namely that tourism "comprises destinations, activities and travel facilitation." The photograph on the page opposite this definition carries a caption stating that "A destination resort must cater to all the needs of its guests," and the photograph to support this statement depicts four guests on the 18th green of a resort golf course. This is but one small typical illustration of the symbiotic relationship which now exists between sport and tourism, where increasingly the "needs" of tourists are catered for through the provision of sporting facilities and experiences.

A British publication of the same year referred to this growing athletic appetite within the tourist industry:

> Developments to supply this demand are burgeoning across the world as tourism searches out ever distant and unusual destinations at the same time the more popular holiday formulae, such as Mediterranean summer sun, are continually developing, particularly in activity and sporting ingredients. (Cooper, 1988)

In the dozen or so years since all of the above sentiments were expressed, the obvious relationship between sport and tourism has developed in significant ways, as those "activity and sporting ingredients" have predominated to an unprecedented international scale; so much so, in fact, that the term "Sport Tourism" has been coined to describe this worldwide phenomenon, and is now in common usage.

Sport has been described as the world's largest social phenomenon, harnessing with ease the attention and energies of millions of people, at a cost of billions of dollars. Tourism has been called the world's largest industry, encompassing the employment and enjoyment of people everywhere through the interrelated use of accommodations, entertainment and travel. It would seem strange indeed, therefore, if sport and tourism did not interact; in fact, their points of contact can be traced back to Ancient Greece, until in the modern world our technology has created a virtual and unparalleled international playground for tourists.

A brief historical overview of the development of Sport Tourism up to modern times is given in the first part of the Chapter 2. The remaining chapters are devoted to the development of the six key areas that identify Sport Tourism today, i.e. multi-sport festivals; sport in parks; sport vacations; sports museums and halls of fame; the emerging role of government in sport tourism; and the growing area of the sport tourism profession. These six chapters examine in turn the evolution of each one of these key components in Canada, with case studies/profiles as examples, where appropriate, and references provided for further reading and study. The whole is intended as an introduction to Canadian Sport Tourism. It is designed to illustrate how Canada is playing a major role in this important international field, one whose significance should be recognized, and that should only increase in the future. It is hoped that it may be of particular use and interest to the growing number of students and professionals, who may be seeking future employment in the myriad of opportunities made available through the growth of Sport Tourism in Canada.

References

Cooper, C.P. (1989). *Progress in Tourism, Recreation and Hospitality Management*. Volume 1, Belhaven Press, London.

Ellis, T., & Norton, R. L. (1988). *Commercial Recreation: A Managerial Approach*. Mosby Publisher, St Louis.

Sport and Tourism Development In Canada: An Overview

Contemporary sport is an international phenomenon of gigantic dimensions which attracts a large amount of media attention. A similar status can also be claimed by tourism, supported by impressive and increasing evidence, which indicates it is the fastest growing industry in the world today. Perhaps it is not surprising then, that a symbiotic relationship exists between sport and tourism. Indeed, their points of contact have increased significantly and dramatically in recent years, a trend which present indicators suggest will continue throughout the world.

In 2001, tourism spending in Canada reached a record $54.6 billion, up .9% from 2000, outperforming the growth of the Canadian economy as measured by the GDP, and continues to be one of Canada's major employment generators. (Statistics Canada, 2000; Canadian Tourism Commission [CTC], 2001). Other noteworthy information regarding tourism in Canada included:

- In 2000, Tourism generated 546,400 jobs
- Foreigners spent $16.2 billion while Canadians accounted for $38.4 billion
- All of Canada's major overseas markets recorded an average increase of 3% in overnight trips from 1999
- Canada ranked 9th in the world as a travel destination
- Total outbound travel by Canadians increased to 19.2 million overnight trips.

8th IAAF World Athletics Championships, Edmonton, Alberta.
(S. Petersen Photograph)

During the past decade, sport has made significant contributions to the economy of Canada and the world through both professional and amateur endeavors. The estimated "economic impact of sport" (Donnelly, 2000) indicated:
- Overall annual turnover: over $400 billion
- U.S. annual turnover: nearly $200 billion
- Soccer annual turnover: over $200 billion
- Annual growth rate: between 6% and 10%
- Share of GDP in rich countries: between 1% and 1.5%
- Share of world trade: 2.5%
- Sponsorship worldwide: nearly $7 billion
- Stock exchange value of English football club Manchester United: $1+ billion
- Ferrari's annual budget: nearly $150 million
- Michael Jordan's earnings in 1997 nearly $80 million

The Sports Tourism International Council (2000) described the development of Sport Tourism in Canada thus:

Sport tourism has been a philosophical impetus in Canada and has made significant growth through the past two decades because of industry initiatives:
- The "sport tourism" phenomenon has been evidenced through worldwide popularity of sports events, such as the Olympics and professional super championships.
- The concept of health through physical activities for all age levels sparked renewed interest in a variety of physical activity participation.
- Interactions between sport and tourism, such as contributions to the execution of development plans, role in promoting domestic, national, international friendship and understanding among people and communities have prompted leaders to foster and enhance specific sporting activities.
- Studies demonstrate a tendency to break up "yearly free time blocks" into a series of short periods. As such, spectator and participant tourists are able to enjoy different sports at different times of the year.

These are just a few of the impacts which sport tourism has had on Canada and the world. As we move into the twenty-first century, the growth of the sport tourism sector does not appear to be slowing, in fact, it is expanding at an increasingly fast pace.

References

Canadian Tourism Commission (2000). *Canadian Tourism Facts & Figures 2000, 2001.* Statistics Canada, Tourism Statistics Program, Ottawa.

Donnelly, P. (2000). *Taking Sport Seriously. Social Issues in Canadian Sport.* Thompson Educational Publishing, Inc., Toronto, p. 19.

Sports Tourism International Council (2000). *SportQuest: Developing the Sports Tourism Profession.* Online Available: http//www.sporquest.com/tourism/, pp. 1-3.

8th IAAF World Athletics Championships, Edmonton, Alberta.
(S. Petersen Photograph)

Chapter I

Introduction to Sport Tourism

Chapter Learning Objectives: By the end of the chapter the student should be able to:

1. Define the terms sport, tourism and sport tourism.
2. Explain the points of contact of sport and tourism.
3. Understand and describe the symbiotic relationship that exists between sport and tourism.
4. Describe the roles sport tourism has played and its' impact in the world and Canada today.

Introduction

The purpose of the chapter is to examine the relationship between sport and tourism through identification, definition and their points of contact. The term "sport tourism" has been coined to describe the symbiotic relationship that exists between the two. To further enhance the understanding of this partnership it is necessary to begin by defining sport, tourism and sport tourism.

What Is Sport?

Sport has existed longer than have written words to record its' existence. Before it was referred to in art or literature, sport had already developed to a significant degree. As will be seen in Chapter 2 (Historical Perspectives) since ancient times, in nearly every place and period, sport has played an important cultural role.

Sport's unique status in the modern world has been proclaimed by many other authors, all of whom have struggled to describe adequately its vast dimensions. In 1958, Alex Natan wrote: "Never has a state risen so swiftly to world power as has sport. It has within sixty years hurried through a development for which empires have needed five centuries". Five years afterwards another analyst wrote that sport permeated any number of levels of contemporary society, and even deeply influenced "such disparate elements as status, race relations, business life, automotive design, clothing styles, the concept of hero, language and ethical values." (Boyle, 1963). To an Australian journalist ten years later, sport was his country's "national obsession," an argument he justified in book form over three hundred pages (Dunstan, 1973); but in reality it is an international obsession, passionately shared by many other countries. The esteemed American historian Barbara Tuchman (1981), illustrated as much with her penetrating statement about sport:

> Homo Ludens, man at play, is surely as significant a figure as man at war or work. In human activity the invention of the ball may be said to rank with the invention of the wheel. Imagine America without baseball, Europe without soccer, England without Cricket, the Italians without Bocci, China without ping pong and tennis for no one.

Our world without sport is indeed unimaginable. It may be regarded now, in fact, as argued in a BBC Series on the topic, as a "universal language — an Esperanto that unites peoples of every creed, kind and color. It is much more than a game" (Coe, Teasdale, and Wickham, 1992).

Although a typical Dictionary definition of sport may satisfy most people, e.g. "1. an athletic activity requiring skill or physical prowess and often of a competitive nature. 2. diversion, recreation. 3. fun" (Random House College Dictionary, 1975), the very scope of sport alluded to means that it defies a precise definition which may be acceptable and inclusive enough for all. Particularly in the social sciences, definitions that satisfy a majority of practitioners and researchers are difficult to obtain. What is "play", for example, or "leisure"? It is easy to find numerous and differing definitions for both these commonly used terms, as well as others in the field, like "recreation" or "pastime." So it is with sport, as John Loy has pointed out in his "definitional effort" of 1969, stating that: "Sport is a highly ambiguous term having different meanings for various people" (Loy, J. and Kenyon, 1969). In fact, two years earlier in what was described as "the first systematic critique of sport theory ever attempted" and in which the words "sport is..." are probably used more than in any other book, author Howard Slusher concedes that the concept defies definition (Slusher, 1967). Although sport may be impossible to define in any universally accepted sense, it is always desirable to have a working definition for the subject under study. Researchers more often than not include a segment entitled "Definition of Terms" which the reader must accept and understand beforehand, for the sake of clarity.

For the purpose of this text, the definition provided by Spears and Swanson (1978) is thought to be the most adequate and suitable:

> Sport will be considered to be activities involving physical prowess, competition, strategy and/or chance and engaged in for the enjoyment and satisfaction of the participant and/or others. This definition includes both organized sport and sport engaged in for recreational purpose. It already includes the component of sport entertainment, which encompasses professional sport.

This definition also seems to be the most compatible when attempting to define "tourism" and "sport tourism." It underlines the authors' belief that sport is the biggest social phenomenon in the world.

Sport has also been defined as a pastime, a diversion, play and fun (Donnelly, 2000; Kelly & Freysinger, 2000). In his book, *Taking Sport Seriously*, Donnelly suggested "sport is about play, games, fun. It is not supposed to be serious; it is the toy department of life." Coakley, (1994), further added,

> Sports cannot be ignored because they are such a pervasive part of life in contemporary society. It does not take a sociologist to call our attention to the fact that

during the twenty-first century the popularity and visibility of sports have grown dramatically in many countries around the world, especially those in which industrialization has occurred. A survey of the mass media shows that newspapers in most cities devote entire sections of their daily editions to the coverage of sport. This is especially true in North America, where space given to sports coverage frequently surpasses the space given to the economy, politics or any other single topic of interest. Radio and television stations bring numerous hours of live and taped sporting events to people all around the world. Sport personalities are objects of attention-as heroes and antiheroes. Young people in many countries are apt to be more familiar with the names of top-level athletes than with the names of their national religious, economic and political leaders. For a large segment of the population, sport is likely to be included in their every-day lives through their involvement as participants or spectators, through their reading, or through their conversation with friends and acquaintances.

Kelly (1996) has suggested:

Sport is everywhere. Children play their versions of sports wherever they can find a little space. Schools require some sport participation in classes and offer a wide spectrum of sport opportunities after class hours. Television has a constant stream of sport programs from all over the world, twenty four hours a day. Sport is organized activity in which physical effort is related to that of others in some relative measurement of outcomes with accepted regularities and forms.

It's easy to see that sport plays a significant role in today's society.

What is Tourism?

Worldwide tourism revenues have surpassed the two trillion dollars a year mark. This total is difficult to comprehend. To assist our comprehension of the annual spending, if you had one million dollars to spend a day, it would take 5,479 years to spend these revenues. Furthermore, the tourism industry employs over one hundred million people world-wide. (OLA, 1991). Tourism is the largest industry in the world today.

Tourism has been defined as "the temporary movement of people to destinations outside their normal places of work and residence, the activities undertaken during their stay in those destinations, and the facilities created to cater to their needs." (Pacific Rim Institute of Tourism, 1989). McIntosh and Goeldner (1990) defined tourism as "the sum of phenomena and relationships arising from the interaction of tourists, business, government and communities in the process of attracting and hosting tourists." One further description provided by *Maclean's Magazine* (January,1999) stated, "Tourism is now our largest global growth industry." It continued to forecast that in ten years, " a billion tourists will be traveling the planet." It is not difficult to understand the importance of tourism in the world today.

What is Sport Tourism?

2002 B.C. Summer Games, Nanaimo, British Columbia

Sport tourism has come of age as we move into the twenty-first century. This has happened primarily, as a result of the growth in sports events throughout the world. In North America it is estimated that two out of five U.S. adults (74.4 million) attended an organized sports event, competition or tournament as either a spectator or participant while on a trip of 50 miles or more, one-way, in the past five years (Travel Industry Association of America, 1998).

The use of "sport as a touristic endeavor" has been a philosophical impetus and entrepreneurial development of the eighties and nineties. Five main reasons can be attributed to these industry initiatives and sector amalgamations (Sports Tourism International Council, 2000):

- The "sports tourism" phenomenon has been evidenced through world-wide popularity of sports events – such as the Olympic Games and professional "Super Championships."
- The concept of health through physical activities for all age levels sparked renewed interest in a variety of physical activity participation.
- Interactions between sport and tourism, such as contribution to the execution of development plans, role in promoting domestic national, international friendship and understanding among people and communities have prompted leaders to foster and enhance specific sporting activities.
- Studies demonstrate a tendency to break up "yearly free time blocks" into a series of short periods, as such, spectator and participant tourist are able to enjoy different community sports offerings throughout the year.
- Present day communications networking in terms of roads, airways, waterways, computerized scheduling, and maintenance technology as well as verbal, visual and printed communication – world wide – are contributing and stimulating to the mobility of sport-interested people regardless of language, culture, morals, beliefs or geographical location.

Sport and tourism both have enduring pedigrees, and first merged long ago in their histories. The numerous multi-sport festivals of the ancient Greek and Roman civilizations, of which the Olympic Games are best known, attracted tourists over the centuries. Today, our technology has made travel much easier and helped to create an international sporting playground for tourists and the modern world. And as much as tourists travel to be spectators at such events and festivals, many, if not more, travel to participate in an ever-widening variety of recreational sports and leisure time activities.

Sport Tourism Points of Contact

Sport tourism is now a valid term because of the dynamic and symbiotic relationship that exists between sport and tourism. In fact, their points of contact have increased dramatically in recent years in Canada.

Points of Contact:

- Sports Museums and Halls of Fame
- Multi-Sport Festivals
- Specialized Sports Vacations
- Parks As Sporting Playgrounds
- Government and Sport Tourism
- Sport Tourism Profession

Museums have long been recognized as enduring tourist attractions and the growth of Sports Halls of Fame and Sports Museums has been quite remarkable. This has been both an international and Canadian trend, underlining a commercial and cultural union between sport and tourism.

The tremendous growth in multi-sport festivals such as the Olympic Games, Commonwealth Games, Pan American Games and Canada Games represents another major point of contact for sport and tourism in Canada. The economic impact of such events is gigantic. Canada has played a prominent role in the hosting of these events and has earned the term "The Games Country."

Business and pleasure travelers are often headed for resorts which boast impressive sporting facilities for their guests, such as championship golf courses, swimming pools, tennis and squash courts, wellness facilities and spas, and so on. Older established properties have felt the need to add sporting facilities and programs to compete for the tourist dollar. Specialized sports vacations have moved to the forefront in today's sport tourism industry. An increasing number of Canadian travel companies and tour operators specialize in a wide variety of sport vacations and tours.

The concept of "parks" embraces the important notion of conservation and wilderness areas protected for future generations. These parks are essential, but so too is human play. Parks as "playgrounds for the people" is another point of contact for sport and tourism. Accordingly, many national and provincial parks include facilities for a variety of sporting activities. Some of Canada's most famous golf courses and ski areas are located within parks. Statistics show that such amenities are very popular with visitors and when managed properly, may have positive impacts on the area. There has been less expansion in this area of sport tourism because of the concerns for conservation and preservation.

With the demonstrated growth in sport tourism in Canada, government has become more involved at the national, provincial and local levels. This point of contact includes areas such as political, economic, regulatory and environmental conditions. As well, new government sport tourism agencies have developed, such as the Sports Tourism International Council, whose focus is on the development of the sport tourism profession.

The final point of contact between sport and tourism is the sport tourism profession. The growth of a professional field has developed over the past decade. Many post secondary institutions in Canada offer courses and/or curriculum addressing the sport tourism phenomena. As well, a growing number of conferences devoted to the topic, have taken place. The first Canadian Sport Tourism Conference took place in Ottawa, in 1998. As we move into the new millennium, more growth is expected in this area.

Summary

Sport Tourism in Canada has "come of age" over the last decade. The developments in both amateur and professional sports, combined with the growth in tourism have created an economic phenomenon that contributes millions of dollars to the Canadian economy yearly. As well, a new profession has been born and will provide a significant number of jobs, academic education and training for future generations.

General Topic Discussion Questions

1. Define the following: Sport, Tourism, Sport Tourism.
2. Briefly describe the points of contact for sport and tourism.
3. Describe the symbiotic relationship that exist between sport and tourism.

Online Resources

Sports Tourism International Council
www.sptourism.net/

Professional Development Institute of Tourism
www.hospitalitytraining.net

North American Society for Sport Management
www.nassm.com

Canadian Tourism Commission
www.canadatourism.com

Canadian Sport Tourism Alliance
www.canadiansporttourism.com

References

Boyle, R. H. (1963). *Sport: Mirror of American Life*. Little, Brown and Company, Boston.

Coakley, J.J. (1994). *Sport In Society. Issues and Controversies*. Mosby Publishers, Toronto, p. 5.

Coe, S., Teasdale, D., & Wickham, D. (1992). *More Than A Game: Spirit In Our Time*. BBC Books, London.

Donnelley, P. (2000). *Taking Sport Seriously. Social Issues in Canadian Sport*. Thompson Educational Publishing Inc., p. 11.

Kelly, J. (1996). *Leisure*, 3rd ed., Allyn & Bacon, Toronto.

Kelley, J., & Freysinger, V.J. (2000). *21st Century Leisure. Current Issues*. Allyn & Bacon, Toronto.

Loy, J. W., & Kenyon, G. S. (1969). *Sport, Culture and Society*. MacMillan, London, p. 56.

Natan, A. (1967). *Sport and Society*. Bowes and Bowes, London.

McIntosh, R.W., & Goeldner, C.R. (1990). *Tourism Principles, Practices and Philosophies*. John Wiley and Sons.

The Random House College Dictionary (1975). Random House, New York.

Tourism Is Now Our Largest Global Growth Industry. *Macleans Magazine*, January 19, 1999.

Open Learning Agency, (1991). *Tourism: An Industry Perspective. History and Global Perspective*, 1st Edition, Vancouver, p. 8.

Pacific Rim Institute of Tourism (1989). *Supervisory Development. Tourism An Industry Perspective*, Open Learning Agency, Vancouver, p. 12.

Slusher, M. S. (1967). *Man, Sport and Existence: A Cultural Analysis*. Lea and Febiger, Philadelphia.

Spears, B., & Swanson, R. A. (1978). *History of Sport and Physical Activity in the United States*. Wm. C. Brown, Dubuque, Iowa.

Sports Tourism International Council, (2000). *SportQuest. Developing the Sports Tourism Profession*. Online available: www.sportquest.com/tourism/.

Travel Industry Association of America. (1998). *Travel Statistics and Trends*, Online available: http://www.tia.org

Tuchman, B. (1981). *Practising History: Selected Essays.* Alfred A. Knopf, New York.

8th IAAF World Athletics Championships, Edmonton, Alberta.
(S. Petersen Photograph)

Chapter II

Historical Perspectives

Chapter Learning Objectives: By the end of the chapter the student should be able to:

1. Discuss the historical background of sport tourism in general terms.
2. Describe the symbiotic relationship between sport and tourism in the ancient, medieval and modern world.
3. Provide examples of how industrialization, technology and urbanization have influenced the growth of sport and tourism.
4. Describe the development of Sport Tourism in Canada.

Introduction

The origins of sport are found in the myths and legends of ancient cultures, from all parts of the world, which portray the athletic exploits of mighty heroes. Space forbids mention of them all, but in the roots of our Western Civilization the outstanding example is in Ancient Greece. In his epic poems the Iliad and the Odyssey written sometime between the 8th and the 10th century B.C., Homer provided one of the first literary accounts of athletics, describing in detail contests in archery, boxing, chariot racing, discus throwing, foot-racing, spear throwing and wrestling. Such events came to characterize the Pan-Hellenic Festivals which later became enormously popular throughout Greece. Over the years, these spectacles attracted an ever-growing number of spectators, many of whom could be described as "tourists" because of the travel they endured to attend the celebrations. Here is the first sustainable link between sport and tourism, perhaps the most credible birth of what we now call sport tourism (Harris, 1964).

13

The Ancient Olympic Games

By far the most famous of these multi-sport celebrations was the one that took place at Olympia, legendary home of the Greek gods, every four years. Finley and Pleket (1976) have written of these Olympic Games that:

> . . . People came in the tens of thousands to the greatest recurring attraction of the Greek world. There was probably no other regular occasion in the ancient world when so many people were on the road (or the sea) for the same destination at the same time (p.55).

And the Greek philosopher Plutarch (46 - 120 A.D.) even referred to "globetrotters who spend the best part of their lives in inns and boats," another indication that arduous travel was undertaken for pleasure purposes (Robinson, 1976, p.3).

Held over five days, the Olympic Games survived inevitable changes over centuries to prove remarkably durable, lasting from their traditional starting date of 776 B.C. until they were abolished in 393 or 394 A.D. By this time, the ascendant power of Rome had annexed Greece as one of its provinces and its growing Empire provided further impetus to the spread of sport and tourism.

The Roman World

Robinson (1976) has stated that:

> Travel received a great stimulus from the easy communications and security of the Roman Empire. The significance of the Roman roads cannot be over-emphasized for whither they went so did civilization (p.3).

The same can be said of sport under Roman influence. The Colosseum in Rome was a four-tiered amphitheatre similar to a modern stadium, and notorious for its various "games," most notably the infamous gladiatorial combats. Another favorite spectacle in the city was chariot-racing held at the Circus Maximus hippodrome, where estimates for the number of spectators go as high as 385,000. If true, this represents the largest single attendance at a sport arena in history. Also, when it is realized that other amphitheatres and hippodromes were built throughout the Empire, and that citizens under Roman rule enjoyed a great number of public holidays during the year — as many as 200 days by 300A.D. — it is clear that the connection between sport and tourism was substantially extended beyond its Greek beginnings (Auguet, 1972; Harris, 1972).

The Middle Ages

The medieval period in human history is often portrayed as the "Dark Ages," characterized by feudalism, constant warfare, pestilence, and superstition; and so compared unfavorably to the preceding "glories of Greece" and "grandeur of Rome." Yet after the downfall of the Roman Empire and eradication of its spectacles, sport continued in other forms. The Tournament became the supreme sporting spectacle of the Middle Ages, in which knights dueled and jousted in front of large crowds. Most tournaments were held over several days, included feasting and other entertainments, and were proclaimed far and wide to attract spectators (Barber and Barker, 1989). It was written of a Tudor tournament in England that: "When all were finally present, something approaching a cross-section of the entire nation was visible at a glance." (Young, 1987, p.76). Tournaments were sometimes held on certain days commemorated by the Christian Church as "holy days" (from which the word "holidays" derives) during which there was a cessation of labor, especially welcome to the peasants who had little leisure time. Ball games were not unknown in the ancient world, but in medieval Europe they became more prevalent and varied, leading eventually to the development of some of the most popular sports enjoyed today, such as football, golf and tennis, among others. The popular presence of sport among the masses is confirmed by the number of decrees by various authorities trying to control it, whether because of the violence involved (e.g. football), or to forbid play on the Sabbath (e.g. golf). But players and spectators alike persevered with their sporting pleasures in the medieval Old World; so that they were well-established by the time of the discoveries in the New World beyond Europe (Zeigler, 1979, pp. 57-102).

The New World

History is often divided into three distinct periods; ancient, medieval and modern. The different labels reflect cumulative changes that have taken place over time, and therefore the dividing lines are debatable. The fall of Rome is often portrayed as the beginning of the medieval period, for example, but when did it end? Many would say with the Renaissance, the artistic and intellectual movement which began in Italy during the 14th century, and extended throughout Europe to the 17th century. Others would lay more stress on the significance of the voyages of explorers to the New World beyond Europe — among which Christopher Columbus' discovery of the Americas in 1492 is probably the most famous — which extended the boundaries of travel and settlement and challenged previous beliefs and dogma. Both factors transformed European culture and customs, including leisure-time pursuits, which were gradually exported to other continents; until the term "medieval" no longer fitted the altered world. So when did the "modern" world begin? If not with the Renaissance and/or the New World, many would argue that the Industrial Revolution, the complex of social and economic changes resulting from the mechanization of productive processes that began in Britain around the middle of the eighteenth-century, is an appropriate starting point. The new technologies irrevocably affected all aspects of society, including leisure and travel, the bases of sport and tourism. But first what became known as "the Grand Tour" also pointed the way to a different world of traveling pleasure-seekers.

The Grand Tour

This was the name given to a convention which flourished in Europe around this time, when it was fashionable for literally thousands of young men of means (especially Englishmen) to travel abroad throughout Europe in search of cultural adventure. Besides offering a kind of peripatetic liberal education, it provided the opportunity to return home with consumer goods not available at home, as proof of one's travel and taste. During the time of the Grand Tour's popularity, doctors increasingly recommended the supposed medicinal properties and curative qualities of mineral waters. Centers of medicinal bathing became known as "spas," after the town of Spa in Belgium, and "taking the waters" became a fashionable pastime for the affluent tourist as well. In fact, a quote from Mead's (1914) book of the Grand Tour referring to Spa anticipates the growth of sports tourism in the modern world:

> But as a resort for pleasure-seekers no place in the Netherlands, and few in Europe, rivaled Spa...During the months of June, July, and August it was overrun with tourists, who came to drink the waters and participate in the gay life. In August of 1768 the Earl of Carlisle writes to Selwyn that he has found many friends there and he adds: "I rise at six; am on horseback till breakfast; play cricket till dinner; and dance in the evening till I can scarce crawl to bed at eleven. This is a life for you. (p.373)

Not too long after this letter was written, however, the Grand Tour came to a sudden end with the French Revolution and Napoleonic Wars which followed.

The Industrial Revolution

Great Britain, the birth place of the Industrial Revolution, has been termed "the mother of sport", as so many of today's sports were codified there, enabling them to be played competitively in orderly fashion. As McIntosh (1963) has stated:

> The panorama of World Sport in the middle of the twentieth century shows games and sports from many different countries of origin . . . Nevertheless, the majority of sports in current practice, and the very great majority of the most popular, were exported from Britain (p.80).

Such export was facilitated through the existence of the vast British Empire, the largest in history, where colonists followed explorers and made the first social contacts in the new lands. After settlement, these territories were often made secure by military means, and soldiers joined merchants, missionaries and others in leisure-time pursuits. To the familiar pursuits brought with them from the Old Country were added other activities peculiar to their new environment, part of the assimilation process by which immigrants become citizens of their adopted land. (The roots of such developments are briefly explored in the second part of this chapter).

The inventions of the Industrial Revolution, for example, the steamboat (1788), railway (1820), bicycle (1839), vulcanized rubber (1841), pneumatic tire (1889), steam turbine and motor car (1884-85), among others, improved transportation and increased social contact and mobility. Such technology accelerated the development of sports clubs and competition as well as the formation of sports governing bodies, at local, national and international level. New sports were born of invention, too, such as automobile racing, bicycling, and rifle-shooting. All sport, old and new, was inevitably affected by other innovations also, such as the camera (1826), dynamo/transformer (1831), electric telegraph (1837-39), telephone (1876), electric lamp (1881), cinematograph (1895), and radio (1901). It is salutary to reflect that "the first flickering commercial motion picture was a four minute film of a boxing match shown in New York City in 1895," for example, or that the first test of Marconi's wireless was to report on an international yacht race in 1899. The inventive urge led to the appearance of television (1930s), a medium which altered social habits, sport included, to an unprecedented scale. The appearance of the airplane (1905, and the jet engine in 1939) revolutionized travel, enabling masses of tourists and others to cross continents and oceans, in amazingly short time and with unparalleled ease (Bennett, et al.,1975; Betts, 1951; Jobling, 1970).

Urbanization

Roads connect towns and cities where the major airports and railway stations are located in the modern world, which underlines another factor which must be mentioned in this brief overview, that of urbanization. Cities have existed for thousands of years but only recently in historical terms have they accommodated the dominant proportion of the world's population. At the beginning of the nineteenth century, urban dwellers in cities of 20,000 or more made up only 2.4 per cent of the world total; by 1950 this percentage had increased nearly tenfold. The change has been particularly dramatic in Western countries, another facet of the Industrial Revolution. At least three-quarters of the population of the United States, for example, are now estimated to live in environments defined as urban (DeFleur, et al., 1973, p.279). To a large extent, therefore, modern sport is urban sport, where cities house the masses of participants and spectators, and provide the sites for sports stadiums and other facilities.

Parks

Among those "other facilities" in the modern city were parks, a final factor here whose significance was extended and underlined by urbanization. While parks' history can be traced back to the ancient and medieval world, it is mainly the growth of cities in the modern world which has created their profusion today. As people increasingly moved to towns and cities which became more congested and expanded in number and size, "urban planning" was elevated to essential status; and soon the need for "leisure space" of various kinds was urgently recognized. The modern city brought forth the "landscape architect" - such as Frederick Law Olmsted, designer of Central Park in New York City, among others - to design parks which offered a respite from the unprecedented onset of new factories, housing, railways and roads. In a telling phrase, used by many others since, Toronto doctor C.P. Mulvany in 1884, described parks as "the lungs of the city" (McFarland, 1978, p.14). The role and purpose of these urban breathing spaces inevitably varied over time and from place to place. Some were decorative and intended for passive enjoyment, while others were used for more active recreation. However, sport soon became a function of many amenities. In his "A Social History of Leisure Since 1600", Gary Cross (1990) has written that:

> . . . large downtown showcase parks were most often used by the middle class in the business districts; some provided golf courses and tennis courts used by the well-to-do. From the 1890's however, social reformers advocated smaller neighborhoods. Mayor Josiah Quincy of Boston (1865-1899) supported gymnasia, swimming pools, playgrounds and free concerts in the poorer sections of the city as a means of combating delinquency (p.98).

Parks were seen by many as an antidote to many of the ills of urban life, almost a panacea for problems facing all classes of city-dwellers. The "rise of sport" which took place throughout the industrialized world was facilitated everywhere to a very large extent by the sports facilities provided in urban parks. Such facilities came to be enjoyed more and more, also, by outside tourists visiting cities, encouraged by city governments advertising their attractions. Parks, including their sports facilities, became as much a part of the tourists' urban itinerary as art galleries, concert halls, museums, and the like.

Briefly then, for the purpose of this chapter, a major result of the Industrial Revolution has been the creation of a global mass-production recreation-and-sport industry replete with specialized paraphernalia, catering to an ever-expanding leisure market (Vickerman,1975). Sport tourism is everywhere a significant part of this world-wide phenomenon.

Origins and Development of Sport in Canada

As with other cultures, activities broadly defined as "sport" can be found in the legends of the aboriginal people of the land that became Canada. The Jesuit Relations might be considered as the first hard evidence, containing the eye-witness accounts of missionaries describing various games of the First Nations tribes. One priest coined the term "lacrosse" for one popular contest, as the shape of the racquet used to throw and catch the ball reminded him of a Bishop's crozier or "Crosse." There were some forty variations of

The Miracle Mile, 5th British Empire/Commonwealth Games, Vancouver British Columbia.

this game among the natives; and a famous painting by the American artist George Catlin (1796 - 1872) depicts hundreds of warriors engaged in one version of it. Lacrosse games were a ritual that often lasted for days, played to restore health to the sick, or to honor dead warriors (a parallel to the Funeral Games in Homer's Iliad). (Morrow and Keyes, et al.,1989, p.45).

The settlers during the French Regime (New France, 1627 - 1760) also observed natives at play, interacted with them in some sporting contests, and indulged in activities of their own. There are numerous references to trials of stamina and strength, such as foot racing and wrestling, and many kinds of gambling games. The indigenous canoe, toboggan, and snowshoes - utilitarian and essential for survival in the North American wilderness - were adopted by settlers, and later used for sporting purposes as well. A white man's version of lacrosse, of course, became a nation-wide sport for all and even deemed the "National Sport of Canada". This occurred during the British Regime (British North America, 1764 - 1867) when sport in Canada increased dramatically (Mott, 1989, pp.1 - 155).

Settlers from Britain could naturally be expected to bring their sports with them to the new land, and to participate in unfamiliar but appealing activities found there. What Morison calls "the first recorded international football match", in fact, took place as early as 1586 between British seamen and Greenland Eskimos (Morison, 1971, p.597). Sport was certainly a leisure-time feature of military garrisons' life in British North America; and it became a regular part of early school and college life, following British traditions (Howell and Howell, 1969, pp.19 - 56). Pioneering and sports-loving Scots could be found in cricket, football, and lacrosse teams alongside other immigrants, but were particularly active in fostering their own favorite pastimes like curling, golf and Highland Games, called "Caledonian Games" in North America (Redmond,1981). During this period the city of Montreal became the centre of a vast commercial empire, the headquarters of the fur trade, banking and shipping enterprises, and canals and railways. Not surprisingly most of the first sports clubs in Canada were founded in Montreal during the nineteenth-century; so that by the time of Confederation (Dominion of Canada, 1867) the city qualified for the description "the cradle of Canadian sport". Wise and Fisher (1974) give it an even wider status in their account of a two-day sports festival held earlier in the city, in 1844:

> Neither in Britain nor in the United States had anything quite like these Games yet been held. Toronto, a few years earlier, had held a number of field days; so had some American cities. But in their size, organization, variety, and social and cultural diversity, Montreal's Olympics were unique - on the basis of them, Montreal has a strong claim to be considered as one of the birthplaces of modern organized sport (p.13).

One hundred and thirty-two years after these 1844 "Olympics," Montreal would become the first Canadian city to host the modern Summer Olympic Games, in 1976, the biggest event on the world's sport tourism calendar.

The Vice-Regal Patronage of sport by the Governors-General of the new Dominion was a unique factor in the history of Canadian sport, its most obvious legacy being the number of trophies still competed for today, among which the most famous are the Grey Cup (football) and the Stanley Cup (ice-hockey). Travel for Their Excellencies, participants and fans to the growing number of sports events in Canada, was greatly facilitated by the growth of the railways around this time. Although transport along rivers and across lakes had predominated in early years, the spread of railways which began after 1850 had the greatest impact in this respect. Up to that year less then 100 miles of track had been laid, but by the time of Confederation a network of over 2000 miles linked the major centers of Ontario, Quebec and the Maritimes. The most significant of these iron roads was the trans-continental Canadian Pacific Railway (CPR) completed in British Columbia in 1885; and by 1900 nearly 18,000 miles of railway track was located in Canada, from the Atlantic to the Pacific Ocean. Railway companies soon offered cheaper excursion fares and "generous concessions" to sports teams and their followers, and later became involved in the sponsorship of sport in various ways. While it is the jet-engine airplane which makes possible the schedules of North American sport today, the foundation for such regular and wideranging interaction was laid on the ground by the railways of the nineteenth-century. Towns and cities prospered by the Railways' expansion and the trend to urbanization mentioned earlier was manifest in Canada, also. The population of the new Dominion in 1867 was approximately three and a half million people, of which less then 20% lived in towns and cities. By 1901, 35% of the population could be classified as "urban" (Mott, 1989, pp. 84-89).

By the dawn of the twentieth-century, therefore, sport had established its significant status in Canadian society. It had also played a significant role in the evolution of tourism in the young country.

Origins of Sport Tourism in Canada

A truism underlining the popularity of mass tourism today is that every country possesses something that people from another country wish to see. This desire became a reality for more people through the Industrial Revolution, particularly by those technological advances that made travel easier, and the increased affluence and leisure time of the lower and middle classes. A *Canadian Encyclopedia* (1988) entry dates tourism here back to the early history of Canada, when writings by early explorers and traders expanded existing knowledge of the Canadian landscape; and early artists painted scenes that were often reproduced as engravings used to illustrate travel books published in Europe. While the diverse scenery of the vast landscape may still be "primary attraction of Canada's tourism industry" today, the article ends by stating that:

> The works of man have been added to these natural
> assets through the development of modern and so-

phisticated cities, and through galleries and museums, performing arts, historic sites, festivals and events such as Expo 86, the Calgary Stampede, and Winter Olympic Games (p.2176).

This confirms that sports events are also significant magnets to attract tourists, a fact which was apparent in Canada's earlier history.

As indicated, we cannot identify with certainty the first "sport" in Canada, or the first "tourist" So much depends on definition. Were the early explorers "tourists," for example? Would their participation in recreational activities during their travels qualify as an example of "sport tourism" in its Canadian infancy? From the preceding overview of the development of sport in Canada, it can be assumed that as sports events grew in number and type so, too, did the number of spectators. As travel became easier more of those spectators would be visitors from elsewhere, i.e. tourists. However, a precise starting date for sport tourism in Canada is elusive, if not impossible (and not attempted anywhere in the literature). In the late eighteenth-century an argument might be made for one popular sport as a catalyst, with evidence from three different regions - in 1771, horse-racing was banned in Halifax because it made citizens "idle, immoral, and gamblers"; a racecourse was also reported in Digby, N.S., in 1787; and a Quebec Turf Club (possibly the first sports club on record) was formed in 1789 (Schrodt, et al., 1980, p.199). But definitely in the next century sport tourism became established in Canada, as a few landmarks will illustrate.

Touring Sports Teams

During the nineteenth-century there were more tours of Canada by sports teams from other countries than anywhere else in the world, a fact not generally realized but significant in the history of sport tourism. Most of these tours reflected Canada's place within the British family of nations, and were intended to solidify the links with the "mother country," often with the active support of the Governors-General. Canadian teams reciprocated the connection, too, with various sporting tours of the United Kingdom. The burgeoning railways were used for similar sporting contacts with the neighboring United States as well. When reading the accounts of such tours it is debatable whether sport or tourism was the main objective of the participants. While the sport competition was obviously the official incentive and always keen, it is clear from the descriptions of the numerous sight-seeing excursions undertaken outside the sporting arena, that the visitors definitely enjoyed being tourists, also. And the novelty of seeing sportsmen from other lands attracted tourists from beyond the particular locale of any arena. A brief examination of tours in different sports provides evidence.

Cricket

Cricket was the most widely-played game in Canada in the first-half of the nineteenth-century, and its popularity was emphasized by the number and variety of cricket tours that took place after Confederation, also. How many people are aware of the fact that "the oldest series of international matches" in cricket, begun in 1844, is between Canada and the United States? Or that between 1859 and 1891, cricketers from other parts of the British Empire - Australian, English, Irish, and West Indian - toured parts of Canada on eleven occasions? Canadian cricket teams toured England in 1880 and again in 1887, also. The England touring team of 1859 played matches in Montreal and Hamilton; and this was the first time that a team from another continent had visited Canada for sports competition of any kind, an auspicious landmark for the future. The English team of 1872 attracted the largest crowds, who came to see the legendary Dr. W.G.Grace, one of the most famous cricketers of all time (Schrodt, et al., 1980, pp.47-48).

Lacrosse

The Prince of Wales had also attracted large crowds to Montreal in 1860, where he witnessed "a Grand Display of Indian Games", including lacrosse. In that year the first rules for lacrosse were published by Montreal dentist, Dr. W.G. Beers, who "inspired almost single-handedly", the expansion of lacrosse, and authored a book entitled: *Lacrosse; The National Game of Canada*, in 1869. Lacrosse represented the young Dominion's own indigenous sport (as opposed to the mother country's import of cricket), and it rapidly gained popularity. In 1876, for example, 8000 spectators attended a match in Toronto between the Montreal Shamrocks and the Toronto Lacrosse Club; and in that same year two touring lacrosse teams from Canada, the Montreal Club and 13 members of the Caughnagawa tribe, played 16 games in England, Ireland, and Scotland. The highlight was a game played at Windsor Castle in front of Queen Victoria, at Her Majesty's own request. A similar tour, again led by the indefatigable Dr.Beers, took place in 1883; but this time politics seemed as important as any sport or tourism consideration. By arrangement with the Dominion Government, tour members acted as "emigration agents" to attract British settlers to the underpopulated Canadian West, and over 500,000 special editions of the *Canadian Illustrated News*, together with 150,000 "sundry other publications on Canada" were distributed at 62 matches played in 41 cities, in just over two months (Morrow and Keyes, et al., 1989, pp.47-64). This could be said to represent the first major involvement of the Federal Government in sports tourism, albeit overseas, another significant landmark. In the next century, as sport and tourism grew apace and interacted on a larger scale, direct Government involvement at all levels became common in Canada, and elsewhere.

Caledonian Games and Curling

Canadian historian Pierre Berton has stressed the dominance of the Scots in Canada's history, stating that: "The Irish outnumbered them, as did the English, but Scots ran the country." (Berton, 1970, p.319). From this establishment position the Scots were well-situated to indulge their favorite pastimes, two of which were the Highland Games (called "Caledonian Games" in North America), and the winter sport of curling. Their enthusiastic promotion of these sports provided important events in the history of sports tourism in Canada. Caledonian Games became very popular indeed throughout Canada and the United States during the second-half of the nineteenth-century, and were the biggest influence on the subsequent development of track and field athletics. The first "Great International Caledonian Games" took place in New York City, in 1867. Three years later Caledonian Clubs in both countries united to form The North American United Caledonian Association - really the first international organization for the governance and promotion of track and field, albeit with an ethnic flavor. Huge crowds were reported in attendance at the larger cities, even as high as 25,000 spectators, many of whom took advantage of the special excursion trains and fares provided by the railways. Since valuable prizes, including money, were awarded at these gatherings, champion athletes from all over North America (and some even from Scotland itself), made profitable tours of the "Games circuit". With their associated parades and pageantry, these annual Scottish festivals were the most popular regular sporting event across the continent in their heyday, until about the turn of the century. By this time amateur track and field had become well-established, and other sports were attracting large crowds also (Donaldson, 1986, pp.23-50; Redmond, 1982, pp.159-213).

The winter climate and geography of Canada were more suited to curling than were these elements in Scotland itself, and the sport prospered in its new environment. From the foundation of the Montreal Curling Club in 1807 - the oldest sports club in Canada still in existence - to the present day, curling has enjoyed the consistent patronage of influential figures and thrived beyond expectations. Writing in the *Canadian Magazine* (6 March), in 1971, Paul Grescoe stated that: "More Canadians curl than play golf, or any other sport for that matter."(p.7). Three years later in *Macleans Magazine* (February, 1974), Jack Ludwig maintained that curling "probably comes closest to being our true national sport" (p.26). A highlight of the sport's evolution to such status occurred during the winter of 1902 - 03, when a curling team from Scotland toured Canada and the U.S.A. for the first time. The tour inspired the Scottish captain, the Reverend John Kerr, to write his monumental 787-page: *Curling in Canada and the United States*, an unsurpassed record of the sport's development in North America. Steamboat and railway companies laid on special arrangements and excursions for the Scottish tourists and spectators; and Kerr's team eventually traveled over 5,000 miles, and competed in eleven Canadian towns and cities from Halifax to Winnipeg. Kerr described Canada as "the Eldorado of curling", and the city of Winnipeg its "Mecca". With the Reverend's vivid descriptions of each locale - and sub-titles like "The Attractions of Montreal; The Government Buildings (of Ottawa): Sight-seeing, etc". - accompanied by a huge number of photographs, his book serves as much as a Tourist Guide for 1903 as a sport history. Indeed, the only unpleasant incident of the whole tour occurred when the Scottish tourists were criticized for "a Sunday jaunt to Niagara Falls", by a Reverend in Toronto (Kerr, 1904).

Golf

Kerr and his party celebrated their first tourists' annual reunion back home in Scotland by playing golf. Had they stayed in Canada until the summer of 1903, they would have discovered that, like curling, this other Scottish import had also become a nation-wide sport for both men and women. Since the formation of the Montreal Golf Club by their fellow-countrymen in 1873 (the oldest Golf Club in North America still in existence), the sport had grown beyond inter-club matches to include inter-provincial and national competition and championships. A Canadian, George S. Lyon, even won the golf event in the Olympic Games held at St. Louis, U.S.A., in 1904. (Redmond, 1982, pp. 214-247). Many of the most famous golf courses in Canada, however, were created after Lyon's victory, in Canada's National Parks (and later in Provincial Parks, also). Such Parks, in fact, were initially created for tourism and intended more as lucrative playgrounds than as wildernesses to be preserved. Mountaineering was the first sport to become associated with the new Parks, but golf, skiing, and others soon followed. Much of the most deliberate and significant development of sports tourism in Canada took place within these Parks' boundaries.

National Parks

The general manager of the Canadian Pacific Railway (CPR), William Van Horne, worked with Prime Minister Macdonald to ensure its profitability. Both were convinced that the Rocky Mountains surrounding the railroad could be marketed as a world-class tourist attraction; and that the hot springs discovered at Banff could rival a European Spa. Their policies led to the creation of Canada's first National Park at Banff in 1885, soon followed by other "CPR parks "at Yoho and Glacier (1886). Jasper National Park (1907) was initially served by the Grand Trunk Railway which became the Canadian National (CN) in 1920. (Banff and Jasper National Parks now have contiguous boundaries and are linked by a scenic highway called the "Icefields Parkway "). Waterton Lakes National Park (1895), in a popular camping and fishing area, was the first to be created without a railway line running through it (Bella, 1987, pp.1-24).

Action followed to develop National Parks in other parts of Canada, especially during the tenure of the Parks' first Commissioner, J.B. Harkin (1911-1936). Harkin directed the passage of the National Parks Act in 1930, part of which states that National Parks "are hereby dedicated to the people of Canada for their benefit, education, and enjoyment." *(Canadian Encyclopedia*, 1988, p.1616). While Harkin emphasized preservation of the natural resources of the new parks, mining and timber leases were still major profit-makers; and thanks mainly to new roads being constructed tourism was becoming an ever-greater source of revenue. For the increasing number of tourists, the "enjoyment" factor in the Act was manifest in the many recreational and sporting activities catered for in National Parks. In terms of outdoor activity, if municipal parks could be called "the lungs of the city", then National Parks could be termed "the lungs of the nation."

Mountaineers were welcomed from the beginning, and Mount Assiniboine - advertised as "the Matterhorn of the Canadian Rockies" - was first climbed in 1902. An Alpine Club of Canada was formed in 1906, with support of the CPR. Other outdoor activities, such as canoeing, fishing, trail-riding, cross-country skiing, and snowshoeing were early favorites with tourists, also. Curling outdoors was enjoyed by inhabitants and visitors alike, too, until the erection of indoor rinks for the sport later. But golf and skiing became two of the most popular and profitable sports associated with tourism in Canada's National Parks.

From a 9-hole layout commissioned by the CPR at Banff in 1910, and a similar enterprise by the Parks Branch at Jasper eleven years later, these two sites were developed by Canadian architect, Stanley Thomson, in the late 1920s into two of the most scenic golf courses in the world. Golf historian James Barclay (1992) has written of the Banff Springs Golf Course, that: "CPR wanted an eighteen-hole layout that would outclass all other resorts in North America "(pp.369-70). And writing of Cape Breton Islands National Park, Nova Scotia, at the other end of the country, Parks' historian Leslie Bella (1987) has written: "The park contains a golf course, at that point an almost mandatory addition to the recreational resources of any national park."(pp.167-68). (The same sentiment would come to apply to many of the Provincial Parks in Canada, also). When Newfoundland entered Confederation in 1949, part of the "deal" was the promise of a National Park for the new Province; and Premier Joey Smallwood demanded that it have; "all the recreational facilities available in National Parks in the other Canadian provinces - such as golf courses, tennis courts, and swimming pools." (Bella, 1987). As a result Terra Nova National Park was created in 1957, within which the "ruggedly beautiful" Twin Rivers Golf Complex was "built in true harmony with nature," perhaps the best-known such facility in Newfoundland. A later golf course building boom in the 1990s is said to have "elevated golf to a more prominent position in the province's tourist package" (Peters, 2000). The same could be said of other provinces in Canada, too, where similar golf facilities have been constructed in recent years for the same reason, i.e. to attract more tourists. It was even claimed in a recent issue of *Golf Canada* (Fall, 2000) that: "golf is the largest industry in the world born of a game". If this is true of this summer sport, then its history in Canada's parks has been an important contributing factor.

Skiing

The same claim for a winter sport might even be made for downhill skiing, again in reference to Canada's National Parks. The author of *Parks for Profit* (Bella,1987) correctly refers to skiing as " big business", involving "large corporations developing Canada's most lucrative natural resources"; and she outlines the development of four ski resorts in Banff and Jasper National Parks - Marmot (Jasper); and Sunshine, Lake Louise, and Norquay (Banff). From their small beginnings in the 1930s, these enterprises were developed to the status of world class ski resorts, attracting not only Canadians but tourists from many other countries. Some Canadian pioneering ingenuity helped matters, too, when in 1933 the first ski tow in the world was put into operation at Shawbridge, Quebec: "it consisted of a rope stretched between a pulley at the top of the hill and the rear-wheel mount of a 4-cylinder, elevated automobile" (Schrodt, et al. 1908). Given Canada's winter climate it is not surprising now to find ski resorts in every province. These popular amenities demand sophisticated equipment for lifts, tow bars, snow-making machines (when necessary), and appropriate and attractive accommodation for millions of skiers each season. The result is an investment of billions of dollars, involving both the public sector (government) and the private sector (business), in what is commonly referred to as "the ski industry". In fact, skiing represents one of the largest segments of sports tourism, examined recently in an issue of Communique (October, 2000), the monthly bulletin of the Canadian Tourism Commission (CTC), with the conclusion that: "Canada is able to compete now with anyone, and we're optimistic about the future."

Summary

The previous statement above can be applied with confidence to the whole of sport tourism in Canada, and not just to the ski industry. From the beginnings outlined briefly in this chapter, and others not mentioned, sport tourism in Canada has developed significantly in several key areas, each one of which is explored in the following chapters. Until very recently sport's role in the history of tourism has been largely neglected; and vice-versa. The symbiotic relationship that exists between sport and tourism in Canada has not been examined fully anywhere in the literature. This text is certainly not a full or final examination, but it represents a start that should be made, and hopefully it will be of some use to all who are interested in this topic.

General Topic Discussion Questions

1. What were the major sport attractions and festivals in a) Ancient Greece, b) Ancient Rome, and c) Medieval Europe?
2. Why is the "Grand Tour" significant in the history of Sport Tourism?
3. How did industrialization accelerate the growth of sport and tourism?
4. Why can the city of Montreal be justifiably termed "the cradle of Canadian sport"?
5. In what ways did parks impact the development of Sport Tourism in Canada?

Online Resources

Canada's Sports Hall of Fame
http://home.inforamp.net/ ~ cshof

Canadian Sports Halls of Fame
www.canadiansport.com

References

Auguet, Roland (1972). *Cruelty and Civilization: The Roman Games*, George Allen and Unwin, London.

Barber, R. and Barker, J. (1989). *Tournaments: Jousts, Chivalry and Pageants in the Middle Ages*. The Boydell Press, Woodbridge.

Barclay, James (1992). *Golf in Canada: A History*. McClelland and Stewart, Toronto.

Bella, Leslie (1987). *Parks for Profit*, Harvest House, Montreal.

Bennett, B.L., Howell, M.L., & Simri, U. (1975). *Comparative Physical Education and Sport*. Lea and Febiger, Philadelphia.

Berton, Pierre (1970). *The National Dream: The Great Railway, 1871 - 1881*. McClelland and Stewart, Toronto.

Betts, J.R. (1974). *America's Sporting Heritage, 1850 - 1950*. Reading, Mass.: Addison - Wesley.

Canadian Encyclopedia (1988). 2nd edition, 4 vols. Hurtig Publishers, Edmonton.

Communique, October 2000, pp. 1 -5.

Cross, Gary (1990). *A Social History of Leisure Since 1600.* State College, Pa.: Venture Publishing.

DeFleur, M.L., D'Antonio, W.V., & DeFleur, L.B. (1973). *Sociology: Human Society.* Glenview, Illinois.

Donaldson, Emily Ann (1986). *The Scottish Highland Games in America.* Pelican, Gretna, Louisiana.

Finley, M.I. & Pleket, H.W. (1976). *The Olympic Games: The First Thousand Years.* Chatto and Windus, London.

Golf Canada, Fall 2000, p.64.

Grescoe, Paul (1971). Any Game Played By 750,000 People Can't Be Dull. *Canadian Magazine*, 6 March, pp. 7 - 9.

Harris, H.A. (1964). *Greek Athletes and Athletics.* Hutchinson, London. (1972). Sport in Greece and Rome. Cornell University Press, Ithaca, New York.

Hart, E.J. (1983). *The Selling of Canada: The CPR and the Beginnings of Canadian Tourism.* Altitude Press, Banff.

Howell, N. & Howell, M.L. (1969). *Sports and Games in Canadian Life: 1700 to the Present.* Macmillan of Canada, Toronto.

Jobling, Ian F. (1970). *Sport in Nineteenth-Century Canada: The Effects of Technological Changes on its Development.* Ph.D. dissertation, University of Alberta.

Kerr, the Reverend John (1904). *Curling in Canada and the United States.* Geo. A. Morton, Edinborough.

Mead, W.E. (1914). *The Grand Tour in the Eighteenth-Century.* Houghton Mifflin, Boston.

Morison, Samuel Eliot (1971). *The European Discovery of America.* Oxford University Press, New York.

Morrow, D. & Keyes, M., (1989). *A Concise History of Sport in Canada.* Oxford University Press, Toronto.

Mott, M, ed. (1989). *Sports in Canada: Historical Readings.* Copp Clark Pitman, Toronto.

McFarland, E.M. (1978). *The Development of Public Recreation in Canada*. Canadian Parks Recreation Association, Ottawa.

McIntosh, Peter C. (1963). *Sport in Society*. C.A. Watts, London.

Peters, Tom (2000). *The Greening of the Rock*, Golf Canada, August, pp. 78 - 82.

Redmond, Gerald (1982). *The Sporting Scots of Nineteenth-Century Canada*. Associated University Press, Toronto.

Robinson, H. (1976). *Geography of Tourism*. Macdonald and Evans, Plymouth.

Schrodt, B., Redmond, G. & Baka, R. (1980). *Sport Canadiana*. Executive Sport Publications, Edmonton.

Vickerman, R.W. (1975). *The Economics of Leisure and Recreation*. The Macmillan Press, London.

Wise, S.F. & Fisher, D. (1974). *Canada's Sporting Heroes: Their Lives and Times*. General Publishing Company, Don Mills, Ontario.

Young, Alan (1987). *Tudor and Jacobean Tournaments*. George Philip, London.

Zeigler, E.F., ed. (1979). *History of Physical Education and Sport*. Prentice-Hall, Englewood-Cliffs, New Jersey.

Chapter III

Canadian Sports Museums and Halls of Fame

Chapter Learning Objectives: By the end of the chapter the student should be able to:

1. Explain the importance of sport museums and halls of fame in Canada.
2. Describe their linkages with tourism.
3. Describe the development of Canadian sport museums and sports halls of fame.
4. Discuss the importance of sports exhibitions.
5. Describe the significant changes to sports museums and sports halls of fame in Canada.

Introduction

Museums have long been recognized as one of the most popular and traditional tourist attractions. They number in the thousands and may be found in virtually every country, in both urban and rural environments. Large cities inevitably have several museums of different kinds, but they can also be located in the smallest village. Their appeal is consistent with their worth in society as specialist institutions which seek to preserve cultural heritage in a variety of ways and in all aspects. (Redmond, 1991)

For clarification, a distinction should be made between the terms "museum" and "halls of fame." The ultimate raison d'etre for a sports hall of fame is the glorification of sporting heritage and the word "fame" is all-important. A hall of fame intends to honor precisely those who are accepted as having been famous and significant enough in sport to qualify. The eligibility rules and procedures for attaining such recognition are as varied as the institutions themselves, but inevitably only athletes of proven ability are elected to a sports hall of fame. Election is for a small elite and visitation is by the masses.

A museum on the other hand exists to preserve all heritage and its' collections may contain artifacts and relics of ordinary "mortals" as well as the famous (or even the infamous). A sports museum, therefore, may display an exhibit because of its' intrinsic historical interest; and the golf clubs, bicycles or footballs have their place regardless of who wielded them, rode them or kicked them. Such objects would find their way into a sports hall of fame only as the implements of acknowledged sports heroes or heroines. There are institutions that are strictly sports halls of fame, others that are sports museums and those which perform both functions in the same building. A Canadian example of the latter includes the Aquatic Hall of Fame and Museum in Winnipeg, Manitoba.

Sport as Part of Museums' Diversity

Not surprisingly, one of the trends that may be discerned in the growth of Sport Tourism is the increase in the number of "sport museums and halls of fame" which cater to the diverse interests of travelers in Canada. Museums now exist which cover practically every sport played today. The status of sport as a modern phenomenon and its' contact with tourism is clearly reflected in the recent and continued growth of sports museums and halls of fame. Tourists interested in sport may now find their needs catered to in an impressive and

B.C. Sports Hall of Fame, B.C. Place Stadium, Vancouver British Columbia.

increasing number of cities and towns. Institutions which are devoted to displaying and preserving the heritage of sport, in all its' broad scope, are justifiably obtaining a more meaningful and significant place among the museums of the world.

The *Big Book of Halls of Fame in the United States and Canada*, 1977, featured nearly two hundred institutions. It indicated that new halls of fame were opening at a rate of one every month. By 1990, one could document the existence of approximately four hundred institutions through out North America. As well, a similar growth in sports museums was experienced during that time. The growth of sports museums and halls of fame in Canada continues.

Heritage Preservation: The Case for Sport

It is difficult now in fact, to think of a popular sport played in our global village that is not celebrated in some kind of heritage institution, somewhere in the world. Major international sports like basketball, football (all types), golf, motor racing, tennis and skiing have many museums and halls of fame devoted to them. When the *Oxford Companion to Sports and Games* was first published in 1975, more than two hundred active sports played throughout the world were identified, most of which had their heritage displayed in pertinent places around the world. Naturally, and as is demonstrated by such examples like the Hockey Hall of Fame, the spectators visiting these sites are sports fans who find another form of attraction to view besides the actual competition itself.

The massive North American predisposition for halls of fame and sports museums may be the largest single contributing factor to their increasing popularity as tourist attractions. North Americans have eagerly preserved and displayed their sporting heritage, with all its' impressive variety, on a lavish scale in recent years. The Canadian Football Hall of Fame, in Hamilton, Ontario; The Olympic Hall of Fame and Museum, in Calgary, Alberta, and the Hockey Hall of Fame, in Toronto, Ontario are all excellent examples of

Canada's preservation of its sporting heritage as tourist attractions.

Canadian Sports Halls of Fame and Museums

Table 3.1
Major Canadian National and Provincial Sports Halls of Fame and Museums

Alberta Sports Hall of Fame and Museum
30 Riverview Park, Red Deer, Alberta, T4N 1E3,
www.albertasportshalloffame.com

Aquatic Hall of Fame and Museum Of Canada
Pan-Am Pool, 25 Posiedon Bay, Winnepeg, Manitoba
www.mber.mb.ca/city/parks/recserv/aquahall/index.htm

British Columbia Golf Museum
2545 Blanca Street, Vancouver, British Columbia
www.BCgolfmuseum.org

British Columbia Sports Hall of Fame and Museum
B C Place Stadium, 777 Pacific Boulevard S. Vancouver,
British Columbia

Canada's Sports Hall of Fame
Exhibition Place, Toronto, Ontario
www.inforamp.net/ ~ cshof

Canadian Baseball Hall of Fame and Museum
386 Church Street South, St. Mary's, Ontario
www.baseballhalloffame.ca

Canadian Basketball Hall of Fame
The Naismith Museum and Hall of Fame, 14 Bridge
Street, Almonte, Ontario

Canadian Golf Hall of Fame and Museum
Glenn Abbey Golf Club, 1333 Dorval Drive, Oakville,
Ontario
www.cghf.org

Canadian Ski Museum
1960 Scott Street, Ottawa, Ontario

Hall of Fame of Canadian Tennis
3111 Steeles Avenue W, Downsview, Ontario
www.tenniscanada.com

Hockey Hall of Fame
BCE Place, 30 Yonge Street, Toronto, Ontario
www.hhof.com

International Hockey Museum
445 Alfred Street, Kingston, Ontario

Manitoba Sports Hall of Fame and Museum
210-200 Main Street, Winnipeg, Manitoba
www.halloffame.mb.ca

New Brunswick Sports Hall of Fame
503 Queen Street, Frederickton, New Brunswick
www.nbsportshalloffame.nb.ca

Newfoundland and Labrador Sports Hall of Fame
Provincial Archives, Military Road,
St. John's, Newfoundland

Nova Scotia Sports Hall of Fame
101-1645 Granville Street, Halifax, Nova Scotia
www.novscotiasporthalloffame.com

Olympic Hall of Fame and Museum
88 Canada Olympic Road SW, Calgary, Alberta
www.coda.ab.ca

Prince Edward Island Sports Hall of Fame
124 Water Street, Summerside, Prince Edward Island
www.peisportshalloffame.com

Saskatchewan Sports Hall of Fame
2205 Victoria Avenue, Regina, Saskatchewan
www.sshfm.com

Skate Canada Hall of Fame and Museum
865 Shefford Road, Gloucester, Ontario
www.skatecanada.ca

Other Canadian Municipal/Regional Sports Halls of Fame and Museums are cited in Table 3.2

The Canadian Experience

In Canada, civic pride in such matters has its' provincial counterparts, for almost every one of Canada's provinces has its own sports hall of fame or sports museum – from Alberta and British Columbia in the west, to Newfoundland and Nova Scotia in the east, and at several points in between – to honor those athletes of each province who have gained athletic distinction in various ways and to display and preserve pertinent provincial sports artifacts. In fact, local institutions can be found which celebrate the sporting achievements of sons and daughters from particular regions within a province, such as the North Bay Sports Hall of Fame, the Ottawa Sports Hall of Fame and the Oakville Sports Hall of Fame, located in the province of Ontario. The curators and directors of these and other institutions formed the Canadian Association for Sport Heritage in 1979 and are involved in promoting sport heritage throughout Canada. So does the International Association of Sports Museums and Halls of Fame, which was formed in 1971. The first combined meeting of the two was held in 1990, at the Olympic Hall of Fame in Calgary, Alberta.

Table 3.2
Canadian Municipal and Regional Sports Halls of Fame and Museums

Gander Sports Hall of Fame and Archives
155 Elizabeth Drive, Gander, Labrador
www.gandercanada.com

Humboldt and District Sports Hall of Fame and Museum
Uniplex, Humboldt, Saskatchewan, S0K 2A0

North Battleford Sports Museum and Hall of Fame
City Library, 1392-101 Street North Battleford, Ontario,
S9A 2Y1

North Bay Sports Hall of Fame
North Bay Memorial Arena, Chippewa Street, North Bay,
Ontario, P1B 8G3

Oakville Sports Hall of Fame
River Oaks Recreation Centre, 2400 Sixth Line,
Bakerville, Ontario
www.town.oakville.on.ca

Ottawa Sports Hall of Fame, Ottawa Civic Centre,
1015 Bank Street, Ottawa, Ontario, K1Y 3B1

Prince Albert Sports Hall of Fame, Communiplex, 690
32nd Street E, Prince Albert, Saskatchewan, S6V 8A4

Prince George Sports Hall of Fame and Museum
Prince George Multiplex, Prince George, British
Columbia, V2L 4V5

Saint John Sport Hall of Fame
Recreation and Parks, Harbour Station, Saint John, New
Brunswick, E2L 4L1

Saskatoon Sports Hall of Fame
Saskatoon Field House, 2020 College Drive,
Saskatoon, Saskatchewan, S7N 2W4

Sport Exhibitions: The Changing Museums

Interested visitors are welcome at any kind of museum and it is because of the modern significance of sport, that increasingly public institutions of different types, not just sports halls of fame and museums, are displaying sporting exhibitions within their precincts. This practice is manifest around the world and particularly in Canada. The National Hockey League, as part of the festivities supporting the All Star Game, has a hockey exhibition portraying some of the history and artifacts of the game of hockey in Canada. As well, "virtual experiences" are created for the fans which place them "on the ice" with such hockey legends as Guy Lafleur, Bobby Orr and Ken Dryden, hockey heroes from a previous era.

In fact, museums have also become much more attractive institutions in recent years, enticing more visitors with a variety of sporting presentations, often embracing new techniques and technology. Museums are no longer the place "bored" visitors go to; they have become arenas for participation and action. Not all museums today have moved to this new level of "heightened experience", and as such they face some of the similar challenges facing other attractions and competing for the tourist dollar. But there is an increased awareness of the issues and the need to develop more efficient and innovative programs and policies.

Without a doubt one of the most impressive museums to be developed in Canada in the last century was the Canadian Museum of Civilization, which opened in 1989. It is situated opposite the House of Parliament, in Ottawa, on a site known as Parc Laurier. The lavish publication produced in celebration of the museum's completion was appropriately titled "A Museum For the Global Village" (MacDonald and Alsford, 1989). Each of the ten chapters in the book discusses the museum in a different light, as symbol, vision, showcase, treasure house, memory, communicator, mentor, celebration, host and as a resource. Sport is an acknowledged "Canadian passion" of the Global Village and may also be viewed in each of these lights. As such, it is to be regularly featured along with other leisure-time pursuits, in various exhibits of the Museum. Towards this end, prominent Canadian sport historians were consulted during the museums' planning stages.

Summary

The explosion in sports halls of fame and museums along with the increase in "sport content" at other more general institutions is one of the most clearly perceptible points of contact between sport and tourism in the modern world. It could be described as a "marriage of convenience" or even a "marriage made in heaven", with no signs of divorce in the future. On the contrary, similar and more diverse unions are expected to be arranged. The wonder is not that this has happened, but why it did not happen sooner?

Case Study

The Hockey Hall of Fame

Sport Tourism Profile: The Hockey Hall of Fame

The following information was retrieved from the Hockey Hall of Fame Web Site, January 2001:

On June 18, 1993, the Hockey Hall of Fame opened the doors of its current home in BCE Place, Toronto, Ontario. The new $35 million facility comprises 57,000 square feet, including 10,000 square feet in the magnificently restored Bank of Montreal building, located on the corner of Yonge and Front Streets, with the balance in the Shopping/Food Court Concourse level. The new Hockey Hall of Fame quickly established a reputation as a world-class sports and entertainment facility and one of Toronto's prime tourist attractions, with over 500,000 visitors in its first year.

Statement of Purpose

The Hockey Hall of Fame was founded in 1943 to establish a memorial to those who have developed Canada's great winter sport – ice hockey. Incorporated in 1983, Hockey Hall of Fame and Museum (HHFM) exists in order to honor and preserve the history of the game of ice hockey and in particular, those who have made outstanding contributions and achievements in the development of the game. HHFM will collect and preserve, research, exhibit and promote all those objects, images and histories which are determined to be significant to the story of ice hockey in Canada and throughout the world. HHFM will carry out its exhibition activities both in the Museum and whenever possible through outreach programs. HHFM is a corporation without share capital and a Registered Charity under the Income Tax Act.

Hall of Fame/Museum Activities

HHFM works with members of the Canadian and international hockey community to ensure that those players, builders and officials who have made significant contributions and achievements in the game are honored and memorialized through their election to the Hall of Fame. HHFM also works with members of the Canadian and international hockey community to promote the game of hockey both in Canada and abroad.

Museum and Archives

HHFM collects and preserves objects and images connected with the game of hockey as it is played in Canada and throughout the world. HHFM maintains an archive of documents and a library of books and periodicals relevant to the history and development of hockey. HHFM acts as the principal facility for research into the history of hockey. HHFM develops and prepares exhibits and interpretive programs to inform guests about all facets of hockey. HHFM develops and prepares outreach programs on hockey, including a variety of traveling exhibitions and a comprehensive multi-tiered education program, to reach a wider public.

General Topic Discussion Questions:

1. What is the importance of sports museums and halls of fame?
2. How do they link to tourism?
3. How have sport museums developed in Canada?
4. What are sport exhibitions?
5. How has the development of sport museums and halls of fame in Canada changed as a result of the sport tourism movement?

Online Resources

BC Sports Hall of Fame
www.bcsportshalloffame.com
The Hockey Hall of Fame
www.hhof.com
Canadian Football Hall of Fame
www.footballhof.com
Olympic Hall of Fame and Museum
www.coda.ab.ca
Canada's Sports Hall of Fame
http//: home.inforamp.net/ ~ cshof
Canadian Sports Halls of Fame
www.canadiansport.com

References

MacDonald, G. F., Alsford, S. (1989). *A Museum for the Global Village*. The Canadian Museum of Civilization, Hull, Quebec.

The Hockey Hall of Fame (2000) Online:Available:http// www.hhof.com

Redmond, G. (1991). Changing Styles of Sports Tourism: Industry/Consumer Interactions in Canada, the U.S.A. and Europe. In Sinclair & Stabler (ed.), *The Tourism Industry: An International Analysis*. CAB International, Wallingford. pp. 107-120.

Shrines and Libraries (1994). Sports Halls of Fame: A Guide to Sports Museums. Review Publications, Ervine, CA.

Soderberg, P., Washington, H. (1977). *The Big Book of Halls of Fame in the United States and Canada.* Jaques Cattell Press, New York.

Chapter IV

The Games Country:
Canadian Multi-Sport Festivals and Events

Chapter Learning Objectives: By the end of the chapter the student should be able to:

1. Define and describe multi-sport festivals.
2. Discuss the importance of multi-sport festivals in Canada.
3. Explain why Canada may be described as "the Games Country."
4. Describe the challenges Canada will face in obtaining future Games.
5. Describe the important "Games" in Canada.

Introduction

The commercial union between sport and tourism is a point of contact that incorporates multi-sport festivals and events within the Canadian culture and economy. The benefits derived from such a union extend beyond the dollar and cents aspect and include feelings of friendship, peace and harmony among different cultures, a sense of community pride, the celebration of sport with culture and the support from the corporate world, to name a few. (XV Commonwealth Games, 1994). To achieve a better understanding of multi-sport festivals and events, it is necessary to examine what they are and the role(s) they play in Canada.

A festival/event has been defined as "a time-limited theme celebration to which the public is invited," (Timmons, 1991). With respect to sports events and festivals, the American College Dictionary (1962) describes them as "a pastime having athletic character; any course of festive activities." These descriptors provide an accurate basis for assisting with the understanding of the development of multi-sport festivals and events in Canada. There are numerous Canadian examples of multi-sport festivals at the international, national, provincial and local levels. These will be discussed in further detail later in the chapter.

Major sporting events and festivals attract visitors and create a "multiplier effect", that is, a spin-off of tourist dollars on the local economy. It is surprising that until recently, little attention has been devoted towards the significance of this point of contact between sport and tourism. In *The Business of Tourism*, Halloway (1989) devoted but three sentences to the Olympic Games, citing them as an "event attraction" and part of "one of the four examples given of specialist motives that give rise to tourist demand". The other three examples given of tourist motivators include the study of health, tourism and religion. Many journalists and academic researchers are now examining and presenting compelling information that supports the social, cultural and economic importance of multi-sport festivals and events.

Canadian Multi-sport Festivals and Events: Tourist Attractions

The most renowned multi-sport festival in the world is the Olympic Games. It has been referred to as the "world's largest mega-event" (Gang Hoan Jeong, 1988). Adjectives such as colossal, gargantuan, and gigantic are frequently used to describe this "supreme" international multi-sport festival. Such descriptions are based upon the impressive statistics involved such as the hundreds of millions of dollars paid for the right to broadcast and televise the Games. For example, one-and-one-half billion viewers "tuned in" to the 1976 Montreal Summer Olympic Games (MacAloon, 1981). The Winter Olympic Games are smaller than their Summer counterpart, but they too have become a larger magnet for tourism in recent years. The 1988 Winter Olympic Games in Calgary, Alberta, recorded about two million tickets sold, a figure which represented a three fold increase over any preceding Winter Olympic Games (King, 1988). It was reported that these Games were responsible for 595,000 visitors, a record number of visitors who entered Canada during the month of February, 1988. This was the highest figure ever recorded since these statistics were first compiled *(Edmonton Sun*, 1988).

It is interesting to note that the Chairman and Chief Executive Officer of the 1988 Winter Olympic Games, Frank King, was invited to give the Keynote Address at the 19th Annual Conference of the Travel and Business Research Association and not surprisingly he focused at length on the Olympic Games as a positive tourist attraction. He concluded by saying "more than a $ billion was spent in the community" and that "they turn out to be dreams of people coming true. You are dream makers when you are in the tourism business and the Olympics business, and dreams of people always have a quality element to them" (King, 1988).

On the surface, this "upbeat image" of the Olympic Games is contrary to the much publicized problems of the modern Games. In the run-up-to most modern Games, there have been problems related to financing, drugs, racial prejudice, political boycotts and security, among others. The 1976 Summer Olympic Games held in Montreal, at one point appeared as though they would not be held because of financial and political reasons. So much so, that the Quebec Provincial Government felt obliged to take control of facility development, and formed the Olympic Installations Board, an unheard of precedent in Olympic history, as the IOC awards the Games to a "city". This action along with others allowed the Games to take place in Montreal. However, the fact that these "successful" Olympic Games incurred a deficit of more than $1 billion has reserved for them a unique but unenviable status in most accounts (Auf der Mar, 1976).

There were some positive tourist spin-offs resulting from the Montreal Summer Olympics. In particular, the city of Montreal was left with a legacy of facilities that have proven beneficial in the long-term. These included the Olympic Stadium, which has housed the National League Baseball franchise Montreal Expos and the Canadian Football League franchise Montreal Allouettes; the Olympic Rowing Basin on Ile Notre-Dame and two indoor sports complexes. The 1976 Olympic Games also led to an improvement in the tourism infrastructure – public utilities, expressways and the underground Metro system.

The final legacy for Canada resulting from these Games was the expertise and recognition gained as a result of planning for and hosting the world's largest multi-sport festival. Since 1976, the city of Montreal has hosted many sport festivals and events including:

- 1986 World Gymnastics Championship
- 1987 International Canoe-Kayak Championship
- 1992 Professional Swimmers International Competition
- The Montreal International Marathon
- The Tour de L'Ile
- The Marche International de Montreal

As well, the experience of bidding and hosting the Summer Olympic Games enhanced the success experienced with 1988 Winter Olympic Games in Calgary, Alberta.

The Games Country: International Perspectives

2001 World Military Sailing Championships, Victoria, British Columbia.

Canada could be described as the "Games Country" for a variety of reasons. Because of a peculiar mixture of history, geography and some political factors, Canada probably qualifies as the most enthusiastic "Games nation" of modern times, and perhaps the one that most readily accepts arguments of their benefits to the tourism industry. The enthusiasm is in large part a reflection of the direct government involvement in Canadian sport, and its concomitant bureaucracy, now unmatched in the western world (MacIntosh, 1987). Consider that the United Sates and Mexico may successfully host and enter the Olympic Games, but do not qualify politically for the Commonwealth Games. Similarly, Australia and England participate in the Commonwealth Games, but are not eligible geographically, like Canada, for the Pan American Games. In fact, many people do not realize that the Commonwealth Games actually began in Hamilton Ontario, 1930, and were called "The British Empire Games". When they took place in Victoria, British Columbia in 1994, Canada became the only country to have hosted the Games on four occasions. Since the "Games" in Hamilton, Canada's record in hosting international multi-sport festivals is unique:

- 1954 - 5th British Empire and Commonwealth Games, Vancouver
- 1967 - 5th Pan American Games, Winnipeg
- 1976 - 18th Summer Olympic Games, Montreal
- 1978 - 11th Commonwealth Games, Edmonton
- 1983 - 9th World University Games, Edmonton
- 1988 - 15th Winter Olympic Games, Calgary
- 1994 - 13th Commonwealth Games, Victoria
- 1999 - 13th Pan American Games, Winnipeg
- 2001 - 8th IAAF World Athletics Championships, Edmonton

The list does not include several other international multi-sport festivals hosted in Canada, such as the Olympics for the Physically Disabled,(1976); Gay Games III,(1990); or the Law Enforcement Olympics,(1990).

Canada has an unmatched internal investment in multi-sport festivals which also contributes to its' unique status as the "Games Country." For a western nation, with a comparatively small population, approximately twenty-six million, Canada's enthusiasm and expenditures upon all types of Games, international, national, provincial, local, is unparalleled. Whether or not the majority of Canadian taxpayers agree with this record may be debatable, but the fact that all these multi-sport festivals have been and continue to be, at different levels, important tourist attractions, is a consistent assertion.

National Multi-Sport Festivals and Events

"Canadian Olympic Games" were first suggested at an Amateur Athletic Union of Canada meeting in 1924. With the passing of the Fitness and Amateur Sport Act in 1961, $5 million was designated annually toward amateur sport and fitness, and in 1967 the First Canada Winter Games were celebrated in Quebec. The First Summer Canada Games in Nova Scotia followed these Games, two years later. Since then, the Canada Games have been hosted at different sites across the nation. The purposes of the Canada Games are described as follows (Howell and Howell, 1985):

- To provide a high caliber of national competition every two years for a maximum number of athletes from across Canada.
- To provide an opportunity to measure the development of amateur sport in Canada, assess training methods and foster the incentive to improve.
- To leave a positive, long-lasting heritage of physical and human resources in the host community and province.
- To increase the number and caliber of officials in the host province or territory.
- To encourage greater public awareness of amateur sport in Canada, profiling some of Canada's future Olympians and the competitions in which they participate.

- To strengthen and encourage national unity through friendly competition, by bringing together athletes from all provinces and territories in a multi-sport environment.

Within each province in Canada, multi-sport festivals are hosted each winter and summer. For example. The Alberta Winter Games feature competition in twenty-four different sports, ten of which are Olympic events. As well, Special Olympics take place at the provincial and national levels. The National Games for the Disabled, Special Olympics and Seniors Games, with their provincial chapters host these multi-sport festivals each year.

Commonwealth Place Pool, 13th Commonwealth Games, Victoria, British Columbia.

As with multi-sport festivals, the increasing volume of single sport events and championships in Canada is so varied that much debate has been directed toward this area. Much of the discussion around these sporting events is directed at the economic benefits of hosting such activities. In the USA, the 2001 Super Bowl was estimated to draw 186 million television viewers for the three-hour event. Revenues, expenditures and number of tickets sold were "hot points" of discussion. Professional sport teams, i.e. baseball, football, basketball and ice hockey, all have tremendous tourism potential and hosting the "All Star Game" or championships brings significant dollars into the host city and province. Canada has hosted several single sports "World Championships" including: curling, lacrosse, a number of World Junior Hockey Championships and World Sailing Championships to name a few.

Festivals and Events Abound Across Canada

The future of Canada as the "Games Country" promises continued growth and development. A recent article in the Canadian Tourism Commission's *Communique*, entitled "Festivals Abound Across Canada", July/August 1999, described the status of festivals in Canada:

> Some estimates have placed the number of festivals across Canada at as many as two thousand. That would include everything from the smallest to the most recognized festivals in Canada. Part of the reason is that as yet there is no national festival organization to compile the numbers and assess their economic impact on the country's tourism fortunes. Individual provinces are active in the festival business. In fact, a national network of provincial festival organizations is being established. The group is getting set to work out an agenda to focus on issues including marketing, establishing a better picture of the industry in Canada and looking at the roles of the players, including local governments.

Another article in the *Communique*, July 1998, discussed the potential for promoting Canada through the use of events. "Events are a relatively new way to market products that are traditionally promoted through the media. When the product is a tourism destination, events are not just an alternative form of marketing; they are the best form, because they allow us to reach the consumer at the lifestyle level to promote a lifestyle product".

Skiing is a good example. The Canadian Tourism Commission is working to expand American interest in Canada as a destination for ski holidays. In 1998 it participated in "the Live Christmas Tree", in New York where, every year, crowds gather to hear a children's choir sing Christmas carols, while choreographed as a moving tree. Canada participated with sport-related, attention-grabbing ski-acrobats. The message? "Its winter. Think about Canada. Think about skiing. Think about skill and excitement".

The final example of Canadian multi-sport festivals comes from the national parks. In January of 1997, the 81st Banff/Lake Louise Winter Festival was held. The event provides visitors with a variety of things to see and do in a spectacular mountain setting. Winter sporting activities included snowboard contests, cross country skiing, the Banff Curling Club's 100th Anniversary Celebrations, festivities recognizing the Upper and Lower Hot Springs, Springs Historic Site plus the Winter Festival Art Walk and Adventure.

Summary

Multi-sport festivals have become a mainstay for tourism development in Canada throughout the last decade. They have increased in numbers, have been promoted for a variety of reasons and for different participants, they cater to an ever-widening audience and governments at all levels have profited financially in revenue from their activities. There appears to be no decline in this activity, in fact, Canada is actively pursuing the bid for the 2010 Winter Olympics for Whistler, British Columbia.

Profile

The 13th Pan American Games

The following information was retrieved from the PanAmerican Games Society, 1998.

Winnipeg, Manitoba hosted the 13th Pan American Games, from July 24th – August 8th, 1999. This event is the largest multi-sport event in the world, after the Olympic Games. The premier international sporting festival was expected to host 110,000 visitors during the seventeen days, which included sporting events, cultural activities and other related events hosted throughout the surrounding areas including Portage la Prairie, Gimli, Minnedosa, Stonewall, La Riviere and Brandon (*Communique*, September 1998).

The success of the festival, last hosted in Winnipeg in 1967, was reported as "modest". The *Communique*, (September 1999) stated: "Athletes, journalists and spectators from forty-two nations of North, Central and South America, as well as the Caribbean, converged on the city of 700,000 for seventeen days of world class sporting events and a splendid variety of music, and cultural festivities". Winnipeg is the only city besides Mexico City, Headquarters of the Pan American Games Organization, to have hosted these Games twice. "It's been wonderful for the people and spirit of Winnipeg," said Penny McMillan, executive director of Tourism Winnipeg. There are dozens of legacies that will come out of the 1999 Games, and you can't beat the positive press Winnipeg and Manitoba received during the Games".

But did all that positive media and hype translate into tourism business? It's too soon for definite figures, but many of the experts don't believe so in the short-term. "I think we have seen more of a trickle effect as opposed to an explosion," said Doug Stephen, president of WOW Hospitality Concepts, a company owning several downtown Winnipeg restaurants. The same held true for the hotel industry. "Occupancy rates were about 90 per cent, only slightly higher than the 80 plus per cent average for Winnipeg summers", reported John Read, executive vice-president of the Manitoba Hotel Association.

Representatives of Winnipeg's taxi cab industry voiced their displeasure with the large number of Pan Am vans donated by Ford and driven by volunteers, who shuttled dignitaries around the city at no charge, resulting in actual revenue to cabbies being 40 per cent less than projected.

Winnipeg and Manitoba put on their "Sunday Best" during the Games and it seems to have been beneficial. The president of the Pan American Games Organization, Marion Vasquez Rana, called these years Games, the "best yet". "Hopefully, that will have a positive long-term effect on tourism in the province," said WOW's Hospitality's Stephen.

Velodrome Multi-Sport Community-based Facility,
Victoria, British Columbia.

Case Study

Amateur Tourism Starting To Gather Steam

B.C. Tourism Operators Have Discovered
Gold in Amateur Sports

The following article by Bruce Constantineau, the Vancouver Sun, November 2000, was reproduced with permission.

While teams don't play for money, players and their families spend oodles of it when traveling to out-of-town games and tournaments so communities are working to grab a share of the market.

Kamloops, which calls itself the tournament capital of B.C., estimates it attracted more than 12,000 participants this year just for field sports such as soccer, baseball and football. That means close to 12,000 families converged on the Interior city. Combined with others who go to Kamloops for hockey tournaments, golf tournaments and other sports, city officials estimate amateur sports attract $10 million to $12 million of direct spending every year. "When these people go to place such as Kamloops for a weekend tournament, they don't want to stay in some flea-ridden hotel" said charter bus company operator Sheldon Eggen, who caters to the amateur sports market, particularly hockey teams. They want a nice weekend away because that's their mid-winter getaway. People do three or four short vacations like that instead of a trip to Hawaii. That's how hockey parents live.

Eggen, president of Delta-based Charter Bus Lines of B.C., said revenues have grown substantially since it went after the amateur sports market aggressively this year. He said transit companies once felt amateur sports teams represented the low end of the market because prices had to be cheap to draw business. That's not the case at all. In many cases you can't even afford to have your kinds in sports if you are not at least moderately successful in life.

Burnaby resident Bob Chapman, president of Wesburn Soccer Club, and his wife, Lora, have three soccer playing children – Taylor, Evan and Natalie – and traveling can pose challenges. Last summer, the boys were involved in provincial Cup soccer tournaments at the same time, one in Kamloops and the other in Chilliwack. Their solution? Rent motel rooms in each city and commute back and forth. "With Lora and myself going back and forth, one of us was at every game", Chapman said.

Tourism Vancouver vice president Paul Vallee noted his organization is one of the few in North America with a person dedicated to the sport tourism market, former Canadian Olympic wrestler, Greg Edgelow. "A lot of these groups may not get very much profile but when you add up all the numbers, it's very significant" Valee said.

A Golden Oldies world hockey festival, for those aged 35 and above, is expected to attract 1,200 participants to Vancouver in October 2001, resulting in $3.5 million in direct spending. A world cricket festival in July 2002 is expected to draw 1400 participants and $4.1 million in spending while the World Weightlifting Championships in November 2003 will attract 1000 people and $2.9 million in spending.

Burnaby councilor Derrek Corrigan said Burnaby has identified amateur sports as a way to attract more tourist traffic to the city. "We know we could never compete with Vancouver for Vancouver-type tourism. People who go to Vancouver to see Stanley Park and the Museum of Anthropology aren't coming to Burnaby, so we had to find a niche". The city has spent million of dollars in developing Burnaby Lake as a venue for a variety of sports and has identified two sites for future hotel development.

A $14.25 million artificial turf complex for field sports has was completed a year ago to complement extensive facilities that existed for ice hockey, lacrosse, swimming, tennis, soccer, rugby, grass hockey and archery. "The idea is to create an all-season complex and we're only limited by our creativity" Corrigan said. "I talked to our staff recently about a beach volleyball center". He said "the future dredging of Burnaby Lake for environmental reasons could also lead to expanded rowing facilities".

Kamloops sport tourism coordinator Sean Smith said the city succeeds in drawing sports tournaments because of its' location, weather and quality of its' facilities. He said the city pays sports groups up to $1500 to hold their event in Kamloops and will try to make the region even more attractive in the future by building a year-round indoor training center for soccer and baseball.

General Topic Discussion Questions:

1. What are multi-sport festivals?
2. Why are multi-sport festivals important to tourism in Canada?
3. Why can Canada be called the "Games Country"?
4. What challenges face Canada in obtaining future Games?
5. What are some of the important national Games in Canada?

Online Resources

World Track and Field Championships
www.iaaf.org
Canada Games
www.canadagames.ca
British Columbia Summer Games
www.bcgames.org

References

American College Dictionary (1962). Random House, New York.

Auf der Mar, N. (1976). *The Billion Dollar Games*: *Jean Drapeau and the 1976 Olympics.* James Lorimer and Company, Toronto.

Canadian Tourism Commission (1999). Festivals Abound Across Canada. *Communique*, Vol. 3, Issue 7, September, 12.

Contstantineau, B. "Amateur Tourism Starting to Gather Steam," *The Vancouver Sun*, November, 2000.

Gauthier, P. (1998). *Using Events to Promote Canada*. Communique, July, 15.

Getz, D. (2003). "Sport Event Tourism: Planning, Development and Marketing." In Hudson's *Sport and Adventure Tourism*, Haworth Publishers, Binghamton, NY.

Howell, L. and Howell, R. (1985). *History of Sport in Canada*. Stipes Publishing Company, Champaign, Illinois.

Jeong, G. H, Jafari, J., Gartner, W. C. (1990). Expectations of the Seoul Olympics: A Korean Perspective. *Tourism Recreation Research*, Vol.15, No. 1, pp. 26 – 33.

Holloway, C. (1989). *The Business of Tourism*. 3rd Ed., Pitman Publishers, London.

King, F. (1991). *Calgary's Day In The Olympic Sun*. Atlanta Urban Land Institute Council Meetings, Atlanta, November 9.

MacIntosh, D. (1987). *Sport and Politics in Canada: Federal Government Involvement Since 1961*. McGill – Queens University Press, Montreal.

MacAloon, J.J. (1981). *The Great Symbol: Pierre De Coubertin and the Origins of the Modern Olympic Games*. University of Chicago Press, Chicago.

Pan American Games Society (1998). Pan Am Games Next Summer. *Communique*, September, 16.

Pendracs, D. (1999). Pan Am Games Provided Modest Short-term Gain For Winnipeg Tourism Industry. *Communique*, September, 13.

The Edmonton Sun, January 25, 1988, p.39.

Timmons, V. (1991). *A Guide To Canada's Tourism Industry and It's Careers*. Timmons and Associates, Vancouver, pp. 232 – 236.

The Victoria Commonwealth Games Society (1994). *Let The Spirit Live On*. Commonwealth Games Society, Victoria.

8th IAAF World Athletics Championships, Edmonton, Alberta.
(S. Petersen Photograph)

Chapter V

Specialized Canadian Sport Vacations

Chapter Learning Objectives: By the end of the chapter the student should be able to:

1. Define and describe wellness, lifestyle enhancement and eco-tourism.
2. Discuss the role(s) wellness plays in the development of sport tourism.
3. Describe a variety of sport vacations and examples in Canada.
4. Discuss the role of eco-tourism in the development of sport tourism.

Introduction

Canadians travel today for a variety of reasons including pleasure and lifestyle enhancement. One of the most significant trends in the past decade impacting tourists' motivation to travel is to improve health and well being. Healthy lifestyles and physical activity have become one of the largest tourism markets in the world. To fully understand this phenomenon and its' impact on the sport tourism industry, it is necessary to explore some of the key concepts and trends influencing an individual's wellness.

> *When a man dies, he dies not so much*
> *from the disease he has, he dies from*
> *his entire life.*
> Kenneth Cooper

Travis & Ryan (1988), described Wellness as:

> The right and privilege of everyone. There is no pre-
> requisite for it other than your free choice. The well
> being is not necessarily the strong, the brave, the
> successful, the young, the whole, or even the illness-
> free being. A person can be living a process of
> wellness and yet be physically challenged, in pain,
> imperfect. No matter what your current state of
> health, you can begin to appreciate yourself as a
> growing, changing person and allow yourself to
> move toward a happier life and positive health.

Wellness is a "dynamic state", that is, it is constantly changing. No one gets well and stays well. Everyone is constantly
changing in one of five wellness dimensions; social, physical, emotional, intellectual and spiritual (O'Donnell, 1986).
The key to achieving an optimal level of well being is bal-
ance, achieved through self-responsibility.

> *He not busy being born*
> *is busy dying.*
> Bob Dylan

Other important terms related to Wellness are health and
health promotion. Health has been defined as "a human con-
dition with physical, social and psychological dimensions"
Bouchard & Shepard, (1991).

> *The only way to keep your health is to eat*
> *what you don't want,*
> *drink what you don't like and do what you'd rather not.*
> Mark Twain

Health promotion is comprised of health enhancing activities in which individuals may achieve optimal health (Epp,
1986). The Ottawa Charter For Health Promotion, 1986
described health promotion as "the process of enabling people
to increase control over, and to improve their health". The
important aspect of these three terms is that they link sport

tourism through the development of lifestyle activities, pursued through tourist sport vacations.

Specialized Sport Vacations in Canada

Many new and innovative developments have taken place in the Canadian Specialized Sport Vacation market over the past decade. Sports resorts, sport cruises, wellness resorts, spas and eco-tourism initiatives have come to the forefront. The development of this market is directly related to the awareness and benefits derived through wellness and lifestyle activities. This specialized market has created a new type of "active tourist" who is pursuing health-enhancing opportunities. The health benefits of sporting vacations, through the pursuit of active lifestyles have been well documented. Benefits include:

- Improved physical health
- Improved emotional health
- The postponing of the effects of aging
- Improved self-esteem
- Improving the potential for reaching life expectancy
- Improved heart health

Haskell, W. L.; Blair, Brill, Barlow & Drinkwater, (1992)

Perhaps one of the fastest growing specialized vacations in Canada has been the growth in the area of sports resorts. The development of golf and tennis resorts, sport fishing lodges and ski resorts has been significant. Many new opportunities and experiences exist today for tourists to participate in a variety of sporting activities. International resorts such as Whistler, British Columbia, have drawn tourists from around the world to come and play in Canada. This type of development has lead Canada to be recognized as a world class "Sport Vacation" destination.

Sport Cruises

Sailing in the Straits of Juan De Fuca, British Columbia

Another recent sport tourism development in Canada has been with the cruise ship industry. Friedland, 1987, indicated " the competition among cruise lines to attract passengers has generated a new marketing twist: sports cruises. Travelers are lured on board by the opportunity to play golf at exotic locations, attend tennis clinics run by world-class players and mingle with Olympic and professional athletes at shipboard cocktail parties". The competition to provide for passengers' needs and interests has meant that specific sports fans are now being catered to in practical ways. In 1989, an advertisement in *Travel and Leisure,* under the heading of: "Athlete's Fleet" stated: "When it comes to sports, just about any sport, Norwegian Cruise Line wrote the book. Our new sport brochure has it all: Super sport football, hockey, basketball and baseball cruises for auto racing fans, skiers, tennis players and golfers. Even a fitness and beauty cruise". This trend, started over a decade ago has spread throughout the world and is evident in Canada today.

The waters on the Canadian east coast and west coast have been attractive as a cruise product (Ministry of Tourism, 1990). They offer a combination of rural and urban coastal wilderness experiences. In particular, British Columbia has become very active in the "access route to Alaska". However, with the development of new ports of call in smaller communities, like Nanaimo, Chemainus, Port Hardy and the central coast, new tourist opportunities have been developed. The newest concept of "cruise-ferries" was introduced by the British Columbia Government in 1996 and has opened access to the central west coast. New sporting activities include eco-tours, ocean kayaking, hiking and other "adventure" activities (*Recreation and Parks B.C.*, Spring 1999). One recent example, The British Columbia Golf Association planned an Alaska Golf Cruise for the summer of 2001 that included golfing rounds in Whitehorse, Yukon as well as other destinations on the journey.

As part of a new partnership program promoted by the Canadian Tourism Commission, The Cruise Ship Product Club and Health/Wellness Tourism Club have been established. The focus of these initiatives is to increase the awareness and interest in these two growing tourist market areas. The industry realized the compelling benefits of partnerships among small and medium sized enterprises. The CTC pledged a three-year partnership with the outcome of self-sustainability after three years. The partnerships were viewed as "invigorating" the tourism industry and improving the competitiveness of Canada as a world-class destination. The Cruise Ship Product Club, is an alliance of twelve partners, including tourism offices, cruise ship associations and port authorities in the Atlantic Provinces, with planned expansion to the other regions of Canada. The initiatives are viewed to position Canada as a premier destination for all-season tourism (*Communique,* October 1999).

Eco-tourism Vacations

Eco-tourism and adventure travel are two of the fastest growing Canadian tourism markets. In 1998, 5.4 million tourists visited Canada's national and provincial parks and another 4.5 million participated in sports and outdoor activities, including adventure experiences, an increase of 12.6 per cent over the past four year *(Communique,* April 2000). This recent growth is but one further example of the impact of sport tourism in Canada.

Eco-tourism and adventure tourism have been described as: "leisure activity that takes place in an unusual, exotic, remote or wilderness destination and tends to be associated with high levels of activity by the participants" (Timmons, 1991). It is "participatory, exciting travel that offers unique challenges to the individual in an outdoor setting" (Kingsmill, 2000). Eco-tourism is non-consumptive by nature and provides the participant with an educational experience.

The Eco-tourism trends and markets in Canada are reflective of other Canadian tourism sector markets. A recent article from the *Communique*, April 2000, described these trends and markets:

> Today, the growth travel markets and by far the largest (young senior and baby-boomers, the 35 – 55 years old bracket) are more wealthy and better educated and want to travel. They are seeking new and more enriching experiences related to adventure, nature and culture. They are interested in soft adventures and outdoor activities, including nature viewing, trail riding, hiking, bicycling, bird watching encompassing a learning component, or being exposed to authentic cultures.

The two largest markets for Eco/Adventure Tourism are the European Market, which includes visitors from the United Kingdom, France and Germany, and the Japanese Market, smaller than the European, but with similar interests in activity choices. The major focus of these markets is upon visiting the national and provincial parks of Canada and learning more about Aboriginal Cultures.

The top outdoor activities preferred by Eco/Adventure Tourists are whale-watching, horseback riding, rafting, snowmobiling, golf, kayaking, dog sledding, snow boarding, skiing and the northern lights. Other activities listed included hiking, nature viewing, bird watching, parks, scuba diving, and canoeing/camping expeditions, fly fishing, rock climbing storm/iceberg watching and snow shoeing. Growth in this new industry has tripled since 1993, with estimated revenue of more than $ 800 million for 1999. There is no indication this trend will diminish and interest continues to grow into the new millennium (*Communique,* April 2000).

The sport fishing lodge industry is one that has experienced significant growth since Expo '86, in Vancouver, British Columbia. Tourists are attracted to the excellent fresh and saltwater sport fishery and the beauty of its' wilderness settings. Anglers have a wide variety of fish to target including salmon, trout, halibut and many species of rockfish. The number of operators comprising the industry is close to one hundred and fifty, with many new destinations still being developed. One of the leaders in this market is the Oak Bay Marine Group, with eight-world class fishing resorts, seven in Canada and one in Cape Maria, Bahamas.

Summary

Specialized sport vacations play a major role in the Canadian tourism industry today. They provide many unique and diverse opportunities for both international and domestic tourists to enhance their well-being through exploring Canadian experiences. The growth in this sector of the industry has sky rocketed. In the foreseeable future, this trend should continue to build and provide significant revenues to the Canadian economy.

Case Study

The Canadian Eco-Tourism/Adventure Tourism Showcase

Packaging Canada's Eco-Tourism and Adventure Travel

The following information was reproduced from *Communique*, April 2000 and focused on the growth of the Eco/ Adventure Tourism markets in Canada.

It has become common knowledge that eco/adventure travel is the fastest growing sector of the world's $3 trillion industry. From east to west (Nunavut and the Yukon) the Canadian Arctic offers a diverse array of world-class features and the packages that make them accessible.

The beauty of the north is dependent upon the pristine setting and element of solitude. This dictates that most packages are aimed at the high-yield consumer with a focus on high quality, rather than volume. Northern operators strive to keep the margins high and the numbers low.

Examples of northern land-based product include facilities such as at Bathurst Inlet Lodge on the inlet side of the Arctic Ocean. Here guests enjoy the comforts of a lodge while spending days exploring the region with trained naturalists and local Inuit hosts. A variation of the theme can be found at Uncommon Journeys, in the Yukon. Heli-hiking among the spectacular ridges is the soft adventure activity. Home base for the evenings is in comfortably appointed Mongolian Yurts with fine dining entrees and wine. Go Wild Tours, based in Whitehorse, Yukon, offers a wide variety of land-based options for guests of local hotels and inns. These include van and 4x4 rides to walking in alpine meadows with knowledgeable guides, beginner mountain biking and custom tours.

In another example of Eco/Adventure growth, Canadian Mountain Holidays takes guests on the most spectacular summer adventures imaginable. Daily helicopter flights take guests to the most incredible mountain hikes; along 9000-

foot high ridges, in stunning meadows or to an ascent of towering peaks. Life at one of CMH's five lodges offering summer programs is as luxurious as the mountains are high. Amenities include: whirlpools and saunas, massage therapists, indoors climbing wall, exercise room, gift and sundries shop. By design, there are no in-room phones or televisions. The library, games area and great room are all hubs of activity.

Each day starts with a gentle stretch class, followed by a hearty breakfast. The guides, based upon personal input, create groups of similar ability. With all the gear provided, guests are ready for a day of discovery. The helicopter is used to transport groups to and from the lodge for each hiking day's adventure – from 100 feet to ten miles and more. There are no trails, but the selected terrain is always walkable, with most of the hiking done above the tree line to maximize the views.

Canadian Mountain Holidays has played host to guests from all over the world, for the past thirty-five years. Their mission is to share the passion for their incredible mountain places and experiences with their valued guests.

Parks Canada has also connected with the Eco/Adventure markets. A variety of outdoor adventures providing memorable experiences for visitors of Canada's national parks have been developed throughout the nation.

In Wood Buffalo National Park, a vast wilderness straddling the Alberta/North West Territories border, and Canada's largest park and UNESCO World Heritage Site, the largest free roaming bison herd is found. The park is also the summer nesting site for the endangered whooping crane and peregrine falcon. It offers many opportunities to explore northern forests, bogs and muskeg habitat, and to observe the unique wildlife. Viewing opportunities are through roads and trails, ranging from short, relaxing strolls, to energetic day hikes and overnight adventures.

The Mingan Archipelago National Park Reserve, a string of islands off Quebec's north shore, protects the greatest concentrations of limestone monoliths in Canada. Sculpted into intriguing shapes by wind, water and time, these huge stone pillars are wonders of geology. More than twenty kilometers of hiking trails wind through the diverse habitats – conifer forests, peat bogs, saltwater marshes, barrens, seacoast – on several of the islands, where wildflowers bloom and seabirds soar. It is a paradise for birders, naturalists and amateur botanists.

Gros Morne National Park in Newfoundland is another example of Parks Canada new Eco-tourism development. The UNESCO National Heritage Site has rugged coastlines, dramatic mountains and majestic glacier carved fjords protecting some of the most spectacular scenery and wildlife in Canada. More than 100 kilometers of trails, ranging from beginners to five-day backpacking routes, for the more experienced tourist, wind through the park. Winter offers cross country skiing and snow shoeing.

Visitors learn about ancient oceans and the collision of continents, discovering arctic-alpine barrens populated by caribou and arctic hare, and explore the 4500-year-old human history, wither outdoors or inside the new Discover Center. Many other Eco/Adventure opportunities exist throught Canadian national parks from coast to coast.

General Topic Discussion Questions:

1. What is wellness and lifestyle enhancement?
2. What role(s) does wellness play in the development of Sport Tourism?
3. What are some examples of unique "sport vacations" in Canada?
4. What is Ecotourism?
5. What role(s) does Ecotourism play in the development of Canadian Sport tourism?

Online Resources

Adventure Network
http/:iexplore.nationalgeographic.com
Canadian Tourism Commission Outdoor/Eco Tourism
www.canadatourism.com
Sustainable Tourism
www.sustainabletourism.ca
Participaction Canada
www.participaction.com
Great Canadian Golf
www.greatcanadiangolf.com
Spa Canada
www.spacanada.com
Health Canada
www.hc-sc.gc.ca
Canadian Health Network
www.canadian-health-network.ca
Oak Bay Marine Group
www.obmg.com

References

British Columbia Ministry of Tourism (1990). *Cruise Ship Marketing Guide*. Victoria.

Bouchard, C., Shepard, R. (1991). *Physical activity, fitness and health: A model and key concepts*. International Consensus Symposium on Physical Activity, Fitness and Health, Toronto.

Haskell, W. L.; Blair, Brill, Barlow & Drinkwater, (1992). *Toward Active Living. Proceedings of the International Conference on Physical Activity, Fitness and Health*. Human Kinetics Publishers, Toronto, pp. 15 – 33.

Pealo, W.G., Redmond, G. (1999). Sport Tourism: Moving Into the New Millennium. *British Columbia Recreation and Parks Journal*, Spring, pp. 21-24.

Canadian Tourism Commission, *Communique*. Adventure Travel, Ecotourism on Path to Success. Volume 4, Issue 3, April 2000.

Canadian Tourism Commission, *Communique*. Health/ Wellness Tourism Product Club. Volume 3, Issue 8, October 1999.

Epp, J. (1986). *Achieving Health For All: A Framework For Health Promotion*. Health And Welfare Canada, Ottawa.

O'Donnell, D. (1986). *Design of Workplace Health Promotion Programs*. American Journal of Health Promotion, Michigan.

Greenberg, J., Dintman, G., Oakes, B., Kossuth, J., & Morrow, D. (2000). *Physical Fitness and Wellness*. Prentice Hall Canada, Scarborough, pp. 3-6.

Timmons,V. (1991). *A Guide to Canada's Tourism Industry and It's Careers*. Timmons and Associates, Vancouver, pp. 238 – 245.

Kingsmill, P. (2000). How Did Plain Old Fun Get So Complicated? *Communique*, Volume 4, Issue 3, April, p. 3.

Travis and Ryan (1888). *Wellness Workbook*. Ten Speed Press, Berkely, p.xv – xix.

Chapter VI

Canadian Parks: Sporting Playgrounds for the People

Chapter Learning Objectives: By the end of the chapter the student should be able to:

1. Discuss why "parks are playgrounds for people."
2. Describe the development of parks in Canada and their role within the sport tourism sector.
3. Explain how parks enhance the business of sport tourism.
4. Describe the benefits of sport tourism in parks.
5. List specific examples of sport tourism in parks.

Introduction

The rise of sport and tourism over the past decade, aided by the mass social mobility afforded by improved travel opportunities has intruded upon parks' space everywhere. Many new developments such as the proliferation of sports resorts and the increase in sport vacations have taken place within the boundaries of national parks. This trend has produced a dichotomy of functions within the parks in Canada.

> A tourist in fashionable golfing togs tees off from the Banff Springs Hotel's new $3 million clubhouse. He swings and the white ball soars over the rushing Bow River, landing on the fairway within inches of grazing elk. This scene, is played out hundreds of times a day at the Banff resort and illustrates the conflict between two worlds, the demands of International tourism encroaching on Canada's rapidly diminishing wilderness and parklands.
>
> Garry Marchant (1990)

The scene described above took place in Banff National Park, one of many such parks around the world and in Canada, with golf courses well-patronized by a growing number of tourists. Golf is only one of many sports in which tourists can now participate in the majestic settings provided by parks. At Lake Louise, for example, one of several ski destinations situated within the national parks in the Canadian Rockies, tourists can enjoy one of the largest ski resorts in the world. To these high profile sports of skiing and golf can be added a long list of other sporting activities which are commonplace in many National Parks, such as angling, hiking, cycling, boating, mountain climbing, tennis, swimming and a host of others. Many resort properties, such as the Banff Springs Hotel, have provided a wide variety of sporting experiences to their guests, through their amenities and facilities, that have become commonplace in the National Park scene.

With these sporting opportunities being offered in hundreds of other kinds of parks, (provincial, municipal and regional), it has become obvious that parks everywhere have become "tourist playgrounds for the people". Given the recent growth of both sport and tourism, such a trend may be deemed inevitable. But it is not regarded everywhere as desirable. While it would be strange indeed if parks had somehow remained immune from the tremendous growth of sports tourism, not everyone welcomes their increasing role in this development. Like museums, parks have always been prominent on tourists' itineraries and have also changed over time as societal pressures affected them. Thus their role and function have changed and have been debated seriously. Sport has historically been featured in this debate, but never as urgently as in today's world. Park use, sustainability and the role tourism plays in the future are part of the new "parks as playgrounds philosophy".

Sustainability: The Changing Philosophy of Parks in Canada

The tourism industry in Canada has moved toward sustainability over the past decade. This new philosophy has in part been a direct result of the development of sporting activities within Canada's parks. Sustainable development means, "that people and industries live within their means in a way that protects resources and the environment". As well, Dr. Peter Williams, an authority on sustainable development, has indicated:

> . . . sustainable development can mean trying to de-materialize the tourism experience so that there is more emphasis on selling value-added experiences rather than value-added clothing. But it is not particularly easy to achieve sustainable development. After all, the industry is fuelled by the notion of people buying and consuming things. We're not there yet, but sustainable development is a state that we should aspire to. *(Communique*, May 1999).

Sustainable tourism is based on the following two principles (Open Learning Agency, 1995):

- Environmentally sustainable tourism ensures that tourism can continue to be based on the natural resources of the country in the long term.
- Both development and conservation can be valid and complementary uses of the country's resources.

In the Canadian context, national parks have been actively promoted for profitable tourism for many years. This historical tension between the use of parks for preservation and/or profit has been actively debated since the early twentieth century. As early as 1917, the Parks Branch obtained the Canadian Pacific Railway golf course in Banff, in order to enlarge it, a move readily supported by the Banff Board of

Trade. In 1957, the establishment of Terra Nova National Park in Newfoundland provided "all the recreational facilities available in the national parks in the other Canadian provinces, such as golf courses, tennis courts and swimming pools" (Bella, 1987). By the early 1980's, hang gliders, bicyclists, snow mobilers, hostellers, hikers, campers, cavers, skiers and golfers were all seeking policy changes to increase their opportunities in the parks. Up until this time the parks use issue was an "either/or" situation. The concept of sustainability had not been considered. However, with the development of sustainable tourism, both development and conservation have become viable options within Canada's parks.

For example, in British Columbia, parks have been actively promoted for profitable and sustainable tourism, a new phenomenon. The province hosts a large number of national, provincial, municipal and local parks in which tourists can play. Many of the national parks host unique sporting opportunities. Two of the most recently sustainable-developed parks are the Pacific Rim National Park and the South Moresby Gwaii National Park.

The Pacific Rim National Park is home to the world-famous West Coast Trail. This "lifesaving trail system" was developed to provide shipwrecked sailors a means to survive the "graveyard of the Pacific", as the west coast of Vancouver Island is known. Today it provides tourists with a challenging, rewarding experience and introduction to the Pacific Wilderness.

The South Moresby Gwaii National Park Reserve is situated in the Queen Charlotte Islands. The isolated nature of the Archipelago is unique with its' native culture and make it a world-class tourist destination. It is the newest national park to be developed in British Columbia and visitors to the area are rewarded with unique scenery, wildlife and cultural enrichment. Sporting activities in these parks include bike touring, trail riding, ocean kayaking, surfing, sail/motor cruising, scuba diving, wildlife viewing, backpacking and guided sport fishing.

Tourism is a sustainable industry, one that may provide enjoyment for many years to come. In the future, the idea of "parks as playgrounds for the people" will continue to grow. Sporting activities through eco/adventure tourism will continue to bring sport and tourism together and the concept of sustainability will help ensure that the philosophy of preserving parks and parkland will also flourish. The two are compatible and form a symbiotic relationship, similar to that of sport and tourism. The key resources that support sport tourism in parks, that is, land, water and air, are renewable and provide many opportunities for sporting activities.

The Benefits of Sport Tourism and Parks

Multi-activity parks abound in Canada.

The benefits derived from sport tourism in parks are as varied and many as the activities themselves. One of the most significant benefits resulting from sustainable tourism and parks are the physical and economical benefits for both the park and the participant. With the development of a sustainable philosophy, parks can flourish and receive a significant portion of the revenues generated through tourist activity. This injection of dollars can help to maintain and preserve the uniqueness of the natural area and physical environment of the park. The West Coast Trail, in Pacific Rim National Park is a case in point. As the park became more popular, environmental degradation began to take place, because more people became aware of the uniqueness of the area, and the demands made on the environment of the park grew to a point where they became a problem. As a result of the growing demand, Parks Canada initiated a reservation system that limited the number and size of parties entering the park on a daily basis. As part of the new system, a user-pay fee was established to support and enhance the areas West Coast environment. The Trail has become a world-class destination and experiences thousands of visitors each year.

The physical challenges of hiking the West Coast Trail are well-documented. The sixty-plus miles of trails test the limits of the most experienced back-packer. As a result, the physical exhilaration of hiking the trail contributes to the physical well-being of the tourist. Having completed the trek, individuals can reflect on the experience and this in turn may enhance their self-esteem through the accomplishment of the physical challenges the Trail provided.

Having identified the first two benefits, economical and physical, the final benefit provided by sport tourism in parks are the social and cultural benefits. Parks are a place for meeting people. They are also a place for experiencing unique cultures. The South Moresby Gwaii National Park is an excellent example of these benefits. Travelers from around the world come to the Queen Charlotte Islands to experience the unique Haida Culture of the area. This uniting of international tourists provides a social union of people from varied backgrounds and nationalities. As well, combined with the Haida Gwaii culture, a unique "heritage" experience is developed and enhanced through sporting activities. Ocean kayaking to the park provides a physical, cultural, social, intellectual and spiritual experience for the eco/adventure-tourist, a well-rounded, wellness encounter.

Eco-Adventure: The New Tourism

One of the largest developing areas of tourism in parks today is the Eco-Adventure sector. It has been described as "environmental, sustainable, high-end and high tech." Furthermore, the Canadian Tourism Commission has indicated "the largest body of tourists in history is on the move and they want adventure from 9 to 5 and all the amenities of home before and after. They want to be alone in the wilderness surroundings and know they are being looked after by a knowledgeable, safe, smiling and humorous guide." Parks provide an avenue for exploration and challenge. As well, they provide protection for the environment. When combined through eco and adventure activities they bring the tourist, park management and tour operator together in a non-consumptive experience.

Prince Edward Island National Park is a good example of the new eco-adventure parks. The park is an "area of unusual sand dunes, sensitive plants and birds. Tour operators need to know how much traffic the area can handle. The only development considered for the park is the kind that sustains ecotourism and respects the park's natural wonders. As long as ecological integrity is the priority, the need to work with the tourism industry is critical. (*Communique* 2000).

Summary

The development of "parks as playgrounds" and sustainable tourism has ensured that parks may be used for sporting activities, conservation and preservation through the development of eco/adventure tourism. This development should provide a philosophy for Canadian Parks to flourish and remain healthy for many years to come.

Glacier stream in the Rocky Mountains, Glacier National Park.

Case Study

The Magic Mountain

The following article by Moira Farrow, *The Vancouver Sun*, March 27, 1993 was reproduced with permission.

High up in a remote alpine valley, you'll find a lodge that combines luxury with a stunning natural setting.

In Winter, ice crystals sparkle on the powder snow. In summer, wildflowers carpet the alpine meadows with the colors of the rainbow.

Year round, guests of the lodge enjoy rooms with views that are a photographer's dream comes true. And every meal is a feast, with delicious homemade creations such as honey-glazed chicken and Jewish sesame seed bread still warm from the oven.

The place is Purcell Lodge, high in a remote mountain valley near the boundary of Glacier National Park. It's the closest thing to paradise you will find in British Columbia.

The dilemma for a reporter writing about Purcell Lodge is that it offers too many stories. Not only does it have superb winter and summer recreation, it's also an extraordinary story about environmental protection. The lodge has spent a lot of money to ensure minimum impact on the pristine alpine surroundings. You'll find everything from a mini sewage plant to biodegradable soap.

Amazingly, the lodge has no road access at all. Everything – from people to paté – is flown in and out by helicopter. Guests are picked up at the air strip in Golden.

The lodge was a realization of a dream for two men who share a passion for mountains and a talent for achieving the virtually impossible. "I saw the place first from the air and I knew immediately it was perfect," said one of those men, 50 year old Ross Younger.

That place was a 2195 meter-high alpine plateau in the middle of the Purcell Mountains, just a few peaks west of the Rockies. Younger had found the perfect spot to build a commercial lodge and they got a thirty-year lease for the site. He and his partner, Paul Leeson, had long talked about such a lodge. Years of experience organizing ski holidays had taught them their clientele was changing.

"The demographics and my own observations are that skiers are getting older. They want a bit of comfort now. They don't want to sleep six in a row when they have to take their teeth out at night," said Younger. He and Edmonton-born Leeson, 37, had previously operated backcountry ski holidays in the mountains around Golden. They housed their guests in "Yurts", round, Mongolian domed tents. In 1989, the men began flying by helicopter to Bald Mountain; the materials for what they hoped would be the most luxuriously remote mountain lodge in North America.

I would not argue with that claim. On a recent winter night at the lodge, I savored a dinner of tortiere and almond cheesecake, gazed out at moonlit mountain peaks and later lay in bed under a soft blue quilt. This is a magic place.

Construction of the lodge began in 1991. The helicopter bills must have equaled the annual budget of Bangladesh. "We used an old forklift scale dating from 1904 to make sure every load weighed 3,000 lbs. Exactly. Those big helicopters cost $1800 an hour so we wanted every load to be the weight limit," said Younger.

To stay within budget, the men saved money by buying massive beams from a local building due for demolition. Then the beams were cut to size. "But our prime concern was environmental impact. We put down boardwalks so that we wouldn't spoil the meadow and the whole thing was quite a challenge," said Younger.

The next hurdles were electricity, heating and waste disposal. Here the men had some luck. A creek near the lodge, which provides the purest of drinking water, also proved suitable for hydro-electric power. This silent and unobtrusive power source now lights up a lodge. "We can run the whole building on 3,000 watts as long as two people don't use hair dryers at the same time", said Younger.

The main energy source for heating and cooking is propane, flown in once a year. But the building is so well insulated and situated that on a sunny winter day the furnaces can be shut down after the lodge quickly warms with solar heat. The small scale sewage plant is so efficient that its processing ends up discharging virtually clean water.

But that is just one part of a bigger waste disposal plan. The lodge also provides guests with biodegradable soaps and shampoos. Low flow taps minimize water use. These efforts add up fast. Younger estimates that waste water from the 30 person lodge is roughly the same as that produced by a typical family of four. "We did so much research on energy conservation that we ended up knowing more than the pros," said Younger.

All garbage is flown out and recyclable materials delivered to the appropriate depot. Composting is not possible at the lodge's high elevation but, judging from the ingenuity of the owners, even that problem will be solved one day.

So much for the technical stuff. What can you do at Purcell Lodge? That depends on the season, of course. Snow is the big attraction in winter. It comes in such monumental amounts of powder that skiers take one look and think they've ascended to winter wonderland, which of course, they have.

You won't find mechanical lifts at Purcell Lodge, so the skiing choices are cross country or telemark, which means skiing downhill and walking up with so called skins over skis. Then there is snow-shoeing for those who prefer a more gentle approach. On a recent morning at the lodge this very mediocre cross country skier headed out across a pristine alpine meadow that made the well-worn trails of Cypress Bowl look like a freeway.

Sitting by a log fire in the lounge (even the firewood is flown in) I browsed through piles of wildflower and bird books, which summer guests use for reference. The lodge keeps lists and photos of flowers and birds guests have spotted. Some guests got so excited they wrote poems about their visit.

Conservation remains strict in summer. Don't even think about picking the flowers. That's a no-no anywhere around here. But you can paint or photograph them all day long.

One of the nicest things about Purcell Lodge is its' friendly, family feeling. At least one of the owners is there all the time to guide skiers and hikers. Some staff join guests at meals, which often turn into fascinating evenings of conversation with people from many parts of the world. Daily in the kitchen, a chef bakes fresh bread and cookies. Breakfast and dinners would bring raves from Vancouver's toughest restaurant critics. Lunch is a make-yourself-a-picnic affair from a table laden with goodies.

General Topic Discussion Questions:

1. Why are parks "playgrounds for the people"? What does the statement mean?
2. How have parks developed in Canada and what is the role of sport tourism within them?
3. How do parks enhance the business of tourism?
4. What benefits, if any, are derived through the joining of parks and sport tourism?
5. What are some examples of sport tourism in parks?

Online Resources

Parks Canada Site
www.parkscanada.gc.ca
Adventure/Eco, Adventure Network
http//: iexplore.nationalgeographic.com
Canadian Tourism Commission Outdoor/Eco Tourism
www.canadatourism.com
Sustainable Tourism
www.sustainabletourism.ca
British Columbia Adventure Network
www.bcadventure.com

References

Bella, L. (1987). *Parks For Profit*. Harvest House, Montreal.

Canadian Tourism Commission, *Communique*, Volume 3, Issue 4, May, 1999.

Canadian Tourism Commission, *Communique*, Volume 4, Issue 4, May, 2000.

Farrow, M., The Magic Mountain, *The Vancouver Sun*, 27 March, 1993

Marchant, G. (1990). The Battle Over Banff. *Western Living*, Vol. 20(10), October 1990, pp. 46-50.

Open Learning Agency (1995). *The Adventure Tourism Industry. Getting Started*. OLA, Vancouver.

Chapter VII

The Role of Government in Canadian Sport Tourism

Chapter Learning Objectives: By the end of the chapter the student should be able to:

1. Describe the organization of sport tourism in Canada.
2. Explain the different roles government plays in sport tourism.
3. Discuss the key issues and challenges facing Canadian sport tourism.

Introduction

To understand the role(s) of government in Canadian Sport Tourism it is necessary to examine why government is involved in this newly-developed field. Historically, government has been involved in both sport and tourism in Canada for a variety of reasons including, political, economic and environmental (Timmons, 1991). Because of the size of the sport tourism industry and the complex infrastructure, it is necessary for government at all levels to be involved. Sport tourism generates millions of dollars annually to the economy of Canada and thus, the government has a significant interest and a variety of roles that it plays.

Timmons (1991) suggested, "The three levels of government have a heavy stake in each province's resources. Almost everything government does impacts on or influences tourism, whether it is setting the exchange rate, building a new port, expanding the parks system, or imposing a new tax such as the GST. Parks, culture, transportation, accommodations, food and beverage, marketing, statistical data, job creation and funding for tourism are all influenced by government legislation". The same can be said for sport. The sport tourism industry is influenced by the government in many ways and at a variety of levels, including national, provincial and local governments. Examples of these three levels are:

- Canadian Tourism Commission – National
- Ministry of Small Business, Tourism and Culture – Provincial
- Chamber of Commerce – Local

Government and Tourism at the National Level

An examination of sport and tourism at the national level will enhance the understanding of the symbiotic relationship on which sport tourism is founded. Tourism in Canada had been organized at the national level under the jurisdiction of Tourism Canada, Industry, Science and Technology Canada, until 1995. Its mission was to promote the tourism industry throughout Canada and the world. In 1995, the Canadian Tourism Commission was created to promote Canadian tourism and capitalize on one of the largest growing international industries to date.

The CTC was dedicated to promoting the growth and profitability of the Canadian tourism industry through:

- Marketing Canada as a desirable travel destination.
- Providing timely and accurate information to the Canadian tourism industry to assist in its' decision making.

The CTC is a unique partnership of public/private sector providing an innovative approach to tourism, one that is industry-led and market-driven. The Commission recognizes that the greatest source of tourism knowledge and expertise rests with the tourism industry itself. Therefore, the CTC, designs, delivers and funds marketing and research initiatives in partnership with provincial and regional tourism associations, government agencies hoteliers, tour operators, airlines and attraction managers.

The government of Canada contributes $65 million annually to the CTC. Private sector has matched or exceeded this contribution and the marketing budget has risen to $145, allowing the sector to compete seriously for global tourists' dollars (Canadian Tourism Commission, 2001).

Canadian Tourism Commission Structure

A twenty-six member volunteer board, compiled from the tourism industry, manages the Canadian Tourism Commission. A President heads the Directors and Chair appointed by the Prime Minister. The Board sets the direction of the Commission through a variety of committees which include:

- Industry research
- Industry competitiveness
- Geographic/Sectoral Europe marketing
- Asia/Pacific marketing
- Canada marketing
- U.S. Leisure marketing
- U.S. Meetings and Incentive Travel marketing

The Board is supported in these activities by the Canadian Tourism Commission staff and tourism professionals. (Canadian Tourism Commission, 2001).

Canadian Tourism Commission Vision and Mission

The Canadian Tourism Commission has developed a vision for Tourism in Canada for the new millennium. It stated: "Canada will be the premier four-season destination to connect with nature and to experience diverse cultures and communities. This will be accomplished through the following Mission: Canada's tourism industry will deliver world-class cultural and leisure experiences year-round, while preserving and sharing Canada's clean, safe and natural environments. The industry will be guided by the values of respect, integrity and empathy" (Canadian Tourism Commission, 2001).

One of the key factors assisting with the achievement of the "vision and mission" of the Canadian Tourism Commission is sustainable development and tourism. The tourism industry in Canada is dependant upon the natural resources of Canada. Good stewardship of the environment will be crucial to the health of the tourism industry. The Canadian Tourism Commission has indicated "The industry has expanded on this vision and mission by acknowledging that, while Canada enjoys a clean, safe and natural environment, the industry believes in sharing the environment with the world, but not in exploiting and depleting it for future generations. The values of respect, integrity and empathy are core values, common to everything the industry wants to do" (Canadian Tourism Commission, 2001). The many tourism opportunities have included:

- Adventure/outdoor and eco-tourism
- Cultural tourism
- Heritage tourism
- Special interest tourism

All of these opportunities have strong ties to the sport tourism sector.

Government and Tourism at the Provincial and Local Levels

Tourism at the provincial and local levels provides significant dollars into the economic development of Canada. Success stories across the nation are commonplace and many opportunities exist for expansion in the tourism industry. For example, in British Columbia, tourism is housed in the Ministry of Small Business, Tourism and Culture. Tourism has been a major economic success story in the province, injecting $9.2 billion in 1999. The province also enjoyed a record 22.3 million visitors during the same period. Tourism creates jobs within the province, in B.C. approximately 113,000 people are directly employed in the industry, many of whom work in outdoors adventure and eco-tourism businesses (Ministry of Small Business, Tourism and Culture, 2001).

Each province is unique in its tourism offerings, with a wide variety of tourism experiences being offered throughout Canada. In British Columbia, there is a world-renowned ski industry. More than $2 billion has been invested into ski resorts in the province to date. With 60 ski areas throughout the province, more than eight thousand people are employed in the industry. This development has been instrumental in supporting the Vancouver/Whistler bid for the 2010 Winter Olympics. If successful, it is estimated that the economic benefits from the Games, during and preceding them, would create more than 25,000 person years of employment and $250 million in tax revenues (Ministry of Small Business, Tourism and Culture, 2001).

At the local level, tourism is usually linked to the Chamber of Commerce. This organization is compiled of the businesses of the local region and many of them are directly linked to tourism. As well, a local association such as the Tourism Association of Vancouver Island (TAVI) is a key player in government involvement with tourism, through marketing, research and other tourism related activities.

Canada Games Pool, Kamloops, British Columbia.

Government and Sport at the National Level, Provincial and Local Levels

Sport Canada is the national government agency responsible for sport in Canada, and is a branch of the Canadian Identity Sector within the federal Department of Canadian Heritage. The department is dedicated to strengthening and celebrating Canada, its' people and its' land. Sport Canada has two divisions, Sport Programs and Sport Policy.

The mission of Sport Canada is to "support the achievement of high performance excellence and the development of the Canadian sport system to strengthen the unique contributions that sport makes to Canadian identity, culture and society". Sport Canada (2001) has identified the following "strategic directions" for the new millennium:

- High Performance Athletes and Coaches: enhance the ability of Canadian athletes to excel at the highest international levels through fair and ethical means.
- Sport System Development: work with key partners to enhance coordination and integration to advance the Canadian sport system.
- Strategic Positioning: advance the broader federal government objectives through sport, position sport in the federal government agenda and promote the contributions of sport to Canadian society.
- Access and Equity: increase access and equity in sport for targeted under-represented groups.

At the provincial and local levels, sport and government are linked through well-developed sport systems. These systems have been established through the hard work and commitment of volunteers, local sport organizations, coaches, athletes and officials. For example, the Sport and Community Development Branch in British Columbia promotes increased access to sport opportunities within the province of

British Columbia. With nearly 750,000 registered members of sport organizations. British Columbia is also unique in that it houses two national sport centers and five regional sport centers under the Pacific Sport Group umbrella (Ministry of Small Business, Tourism and Culture, 2001).

The Canadian Sport System

The sport system in Canada is made up of many organizations that provide sport programming and services at the national, provincial and municipal level. These groups serve either individual sports or cater to numerous sports sharing common needs, i.e. multi-sports. Basketball Canada would be an example of the first, while the Canadian Wheelchair Sport Association is an example of the latter. These organizations receive financial support from governments, according to the scope of their programs. For example, the municipality might fund a local amateur swim club, whereas the organization responsible for the national swim team competing internationally would be eligible to receive federal government funding. National sport organizations also obtain corporate financing through sponsorship agreements and generate revenue themselves through other sources including fund-raising and membership fees.

National Sport Organizations (NSOs) are members of International Federations that establish the rules of the sport and, among other things, determine where their respective international competitions will be held. The Canadian Olympic Committee (COC), is the largest private sector funder of high-performance sport in Canada (Sport Canada, 2001).

Sport Canada has numerous initiatives and programs they are involved with including:

- National Sport Centers
- National Sport Organizations and Multi-sport Organization Support Program
- Athletic Assistance Program
- Hosting Support Program

- Domestic Support Program
- Canada's Doping Control Program

Athletes supported by Sport Canada compete in a variety of Games and Sporting Events including:

- 2001 Canada Summer Games, London
- 4th Jeux de la Francophonie 2001, Ottawa-Hull
- ITU Triathlon World Championships 2001, Edmonton, Alberta
- 8th World Championship in Athletics 2001, Edmonton
- 2001 Commonwealth Games, Manchester
- 2002 Winter Olympics, Salt Lake City
- 2004 Summer Olympics, Athens

Sport and Politics: The Government Connection

In today's society, sport and government have become more inter-dependent because of the important role sport plays in our communities. Coakley, (1994) suggested "sports are a part of people's lives and in fact, in most industrial countries, are clearly connected to major social spheres such as family, education, politics, economics and religion". This description helps in understanding the relationship and role(s) of sport and government. He further indicated, "Sport events and activities require sponsorship, organization, facilities – all of which depend upon resources that frequently go beyond the means of individuals. For example, sport facilities are often so expensive that regional and national governments may be the only organizations with the power and the capital to build and maintain them". Coakley identified six categories for government involvement in sports:

1. To safeguard the public order.
2. To maintain and develop fitness and physical abilities among citizens.
3. To promote the prestige of a community or nation.
4. To promote sense of identity, belonging and unity among citizens.

5. To emphasize values and orientations consistent with dominant political ideology in a country or society.
6. To increase citizens' support of individual political leaders and government itself.

These areas of government involvement clearly establish the relationship and roles government plays with sport in Canada.

Sport Tourism and Government

The sport tourism sector is relatively new to Canada and is still in the "infancy" stages. The next decade should provide steady growth, as the potential for the industry is great. One of the more recent developments to have taken place in Canada is the development of the Canadian Sport Tourism Alliance, in January 2001.

The Canadian Sport Tourism Alliance is an industry-led, market-driven and research-based organization that currently includes over thirty municipalities across Canada. The organization has established a partnership with the Canadian Tourism Commission and is funded as part of the Product Club initiatives. The mission of the organization is to increase Canadian capacity and competitiveness in hosting national and international sporting events. The goals of the CSTA are to:

- Facilitate communication between sport and tourism sectors.
- Share "best practices" approaches to bid models and processes.
- Gather industry intelligence internationally.
- Ensure the high quality delivery of event management services.
- Build investment from the public and private sectors.
- Establish targets for the future expansion of the industry.

The sport tourism industry is estimated to be valued at $1.3 billion annually to the Canadian economy. Furthermore, Canada has the potential to host 200,000 sporting events and games annually and provides significant economic benefits to the host communities (Canadian Tourism Commission, 2001).

Canadian Sport Tourism in the Future

Sport tourism is a vast and growing enterprise whose significance is not fully appreciated. As sport and tourism development continues in Canada, its importance will come to the forefront. With respect to challenges and issues for the future, there are several which may impact this new sector including:

- Economic challenges such as government funding for programs and facilities, consumerism and who can afford sport tourism.
- Societal challenges around the ideas of participation and spectators.
- Industry growth and the rate at which the growth will take place.
- Recognition of the industry as a key contributor to the development of Canada as a nation.

Summary

The relationship between sport and tourism will become more prominent from a variety of perspectives in the future. The symbiotic relationship will strengthen and this worldwide trend will continue to grow and flourish in Canada.

General Topic Discussion Questions:

1. How are sport, tourism and sport tourism organized in Canada?
2. What role(s) does government play in the development of sport tourism in Canada?
3. What are some of the key issues and challenges facing the future of sport tourism in Canada?

Online Resources

Sport Canada
www.pch.gc.ca/sportcanada/SC
Canada Games
www.canadagames.ca
British Columbia Summer Games
www.bcgames.org
Canadian Sport Tourism Alliance
www.canadiansporttourism.com

References

Coakley, J.J. (1994). *Sport In Society. Issues and Controversies.* Mosby Publishers, Toronto, pp. 358 – 368.

Canadian Tourism Commission (2001) Online Available: http// www.canadatourism.com

Ministry of Small Business, Tourism, Culture (2001) Online Available: http//www.hellobc.com

Sport Canada (2001) Online Available: http// www.pch.gc.ca/progs/sc/mission/org-sport-canada_e.cfm

Timmons, V. (1991). *A Guide To Canada's Tourism Industry and It's Careers.* Timmons and Associates, Vancouver, pp. 67 – 86.

8th IAAF World Athletics Championships, Edmonton, Alberta.
(S. Petersen Photograph)

Chapter VIII

The Sport Tourism Profession: Canadian Initiatives

Chapter Learning Objectives: By the end of the chapter the student should be able to:

1. Describe the development of the sport tourism profession in Canada.
2. Describe the growth of sport tourism conferences in Canada.
3. Discuss the development of sport tourism in Canadian academe.

Introduction

With the development of the worldwide "sport tourism" trend, an emerging profession has been growing and developing at an increasingly fast pace. This international provision of sporting facilities and experiences for the needs of tourists has created a demand for research, information and career designation for the sport tourism sector. In response to this need, Canada has become a leader in the sport tourism profession, with the development of the Sports Tourism International Council, established in 1990 and located in Ottawa, Ontario.

The Sports Tourism International Council

The purpose of the Council is to establish a professional association for sports tourism, to foster research on the role of sports tourism and to interlink tourism and sport organizations, groups and other sectors directly and indirectly related to the sports tourism industry. The Council has established the following objectives:

• To establish a research unit for identifying knowledge and understanding of the sport tourism phenomenon.

- To develop a database for sport tourism research and application documentation.
- To host an annual conference for discussion, research analysis and information presentation.
- To establish a Journal of Sport Tourism.
- To offer training and academic programs leading to Certificates, Diplomas and degrees in sport tourism.

STIC has a membership of over two thousand individuals and has an advisory council with representatives from over twenty nations (Sports Tourism International Council, 2001).

Sports Tourism Professional Activities Development

The Sport Tourism International Council has undertaken significant initiatives to establish the sport tourism profession including:

- Information sharing through a system established for professionals, academics and students.
- The establishment of an Annual Conference, that was initiated in 1993.
- The establishment of the Journal of Sport Tourism, a quarterly publication which shares article on sport tourism.

As well, the Council has developed educational programs at the certificate and degree levels. Many universities and colleges in Canada have sport and tourism management programs, with some courses in sport tourism, but the Council has developed specific degree initiatives in sport tourism. The certificate program was developed to contribute to the growth of the sport tourism professional, through education and training.

The degree programs in sport tourism are offered at the associate, bachelors', masters' and doctorate level. Through partnering with the Department of Tourism and CSM Institute of Graduate Studies, a program of Sports Tourism Management, with specializations in Sports Events, Sports

Tours, Sport Attractions, Sports Resorts and Sport Cruises has been offered. Program studies are offered through distance learning by international faculty with expertise in the sport tourism sector (Sports Tourism International Council, 2001).

The Certificate in Sports Tourism Management is offered providing professionals with education and training in six foundation sport tourism courses and four areas of specialization. This program has also been offered through distance learning.

The Consortium for Sports Tourism Education

The Consortium for Sports Tourism Education was designed to enable the offering of the educational programs of the Council in several languages. The initiative brought together diverse educational institutions of higher learning and shares a common interest in the sports tourism area. The Consortium has continued to investigate the potential partnering of the Certificate Program in Sports Tourism.

The Sports Tourism Research Unit

The final initiative of STIC has been the development of a Research Unit focusing on the ever-evolving Sport Tourism sector. The Research Council has contributed to the Journal of Sport Tourism and has examined several issues in the Sport Tourism field including:

- Historical Foundations of Sport Tourism.
- Sport Tourism Management.
- The Development of Professional Sport Tourism Models.
- Motivation and Sport Tourists.
- Economic impacts of Sport Tourism.

As well, a Database on Sport Tourism has been established providing information on five sport tourism activity categories. The structure of the unit is comprised of international researchers from six nations including Canada, United States, Australia, The United Kingdom, India and South Africa (Sports Tourism International Council, 2001).

The Development of Sport Tourism in Canadian Post Secondary Institutions

As the Sport Tourism profession has grown over the past decade Canadian post secondary institutions have responded through the development of educational offerings at both the undergraduate and graduate levels. These opportunities exist throughout Canada and provide individuals with programs of study in sport and tourism management, with specializations or concentrations in a variety of sport tourism areas.

2002 Canadian Congress on Leisure Research,
Edmonton, Alberta (CCLR Photograph).

Table 8.1
Sport Tourism Offerings in Canadian Post Secondary Institution

University	Sport Management	Tourism Management
University of British Columbia	x, y	
British Columbia Open University		x
University College of the Cariboo		x
Malaspina University College		x
University of Northern British Columbia		x
University of Victoria	x	x
University of Alberta	y	
University of Calgary		x
Mount Royal College	x	
University of Regina	x, y	
Brock University	x	x
University of Guelph		x
Lakehead University		x
Laurentian University	x	
Ryerson Polytechnic University		x
University of Western Ontario	x, y	
University of Windsor	x, y	
York University	x	
University of New Brunswick		x
Acadia University	x	x
University College of Cape Breton		x
Mount Saint Vincent University		x
x – Undergraduate degree		y – Graduate degree

Sport Tourism Conferences and Conventions in Canada

The importance of conferences and conventions and the contributions they make to the Canadian tourism industry are well-documented. Timmons (1991) indicated:

> There has been a worldwide increase in the need to hold conventions and conferences. Today we are in the "Information Age" and information is power! Remaining current in one's field is essential. As we move away from a production-oriented society to a technological one, we need to communicate more rapidly, because knowledge is changing so rapidly. As a result, people in all types of organizations need to keep up-to-date. One of the ways is to form associations or societies as a vehicle for staying in touch and communicating information. Besides publishing newsletters, these organizations invite their membership to meet regularly.

In 2000, convention fees in Canada contributed $111 million to the tourism industry, up 5% from the previous year (Canadian Tourism Commission, 2001). The top five convention cities in Canada have been Toronto, Montreal, Vancouver, Quebec City and Ottawa (Timmons, 1991) and this trend has continued into the new decade.

The first Canadian Sport Tourism conference was initiated in 1993. Prior to this time abstracts and presentations on sport tourism topics surfaced at sport management conferences such as the North American Society for Sport Management and tourism management conferences such as the World Tourism Association. In 1996, the first "Virtual Sport Tourism Conference" was held and included sessions on sport tourism research, experiential applications and discussion (Sports Tourism International Council, 2002).

Summary

The development of the sport tourism profession in Canada will become increasingly important in the future. Field-based research and the dissemination of the findings will be critical to the profession. Closely linked to this process will be the education and training of future professionals. Post secondary institutions will need to change with the demands from this new and expanding tourism sector. Lastly, the profession through conferences and conventions must ensure the most recent information is provided to individuals to ensure they remain current with sport tourism practice. Canada can remain a world leader in the Sport Tourism profession through innovation and development in these critical areas.

General Topic Discussion Questions:

1. How has the sport tourism profession developed in the Canada?
2. What opportunities exist for the study of sport tourism in Canada?
3. Why are conferences and conventions important in the sport tourism profession?

Web Resources

Canadian Tourism Commission
www.canadatourism.com
Sport Tourism International Council
www.sportquest.com
Association of Universities and Colleges of Canada
www.aucc.ca

References

Canadian Tourism Commission (2001). *National Tourism Indicators*. Quarterly Estimates, Third Quarter 2001, Statistics Canada, Ottawa.

Sports Tourism International Council (2001). *SportQuest: Developing the Sports Tourism Profession*.
Online Available:http//www.sportquest.com/tourism/

Timmons, V. (1991). *A Guide To Canada's Tourism Industry and It's Careers*. Timmons and Associates, Vancouver, pp. 204 – 205.

Chapter IX

Postscript:
Sport Tourism After September 11, 2001

Introduction

Much of this text was completed before the horrific events of September 11, 2001, when an attack by terrorists on the United States of America was said by many commentators to have "changed the world", and permanently created a different environment for everyone in the future. On that date, two hijacked aircraft flew into the World Trade Centre in New York and another into the Pentagon in Washington D.C. A fourth airplane, perhaps targeted at Camp David, crashed into a Pennsylvania field.

American Airlines Flight 111 had left Boston for Los Angeles at 7:45am with 92 passengers on board, an hour later it crashed into the North Tower of the World Trade Centre. Twenty minutes later United Airlines Flight 175 with 75 passengers on route to Los Angeles from Boston crashed into the South Tower of the World Trade Centre. The resulting explosions and devastating fires caused both Towers to collapse, creating an avalanche of destruction, a mountainous layer of ash and rubble which became known as "ground zero". It was estimated that more than 3000 civilian workers and public safety personnel were killed by the sabotage. Shortly after, it was established that the al-Qaeda network, a terrorist organization led by Osama bin Laden, was responsible for the attack. Since then a coalition of nations from around the world, formed by the United States, has declared an international "war on terrorism". Coalition forces are now stationed in Afghanistan for an indefinite period, while trying to bring to justice the perpetrators of the September atrocities in New York.

The attacks deliberately targeted the financial heart of the United States, causing major stock exchanges to close for days and accelerated the economic recession in North America, Asia and Western Europe. Few economies escaped the fallout from the damage of "9/11". While terrorism itself is not a new phenomenon in the modern world, this latest atrocity represented an unprecedented scale. Authorities were quick to suggest that similar attacks could be expected in the near future, causing a ripple effect of caution and pessimism. This understandable negative attitude was prevalent everywhere, and the sport and tourism industries suffered immediately.

Impacts on Sport and Tourism

Not surprisingly, many people were reluctant to travel, especially by air. Many airlines found themselves in severe financial difficulty after "9/11", with several going out of business with the significant decline in passengers. Since tourism ultimately depends upon travel, the industry was one of the hardest hit by this sudden change in travel behaviour. The ripple effect spread from cancellations of air flights to cancellations in tourist accommodations, rental cars, tours, and entertainment, food and beverage sectors. Millions of potential tourists decided to forgo travel and stay home instead. It was not business or play-as-usual, and the economy of the United States and its' many trading partners were adversely affected.

Participants and spectators were in no mood for sport at this time either. Many sporting events were cancelled and/or postponed after the events of September 11. It was necessary to pause, reflect and observe a decent period of mourning for the victims before any thought could be given to the normal sporting calendar. Even the fiercest competitors and most loyal fans were obliged to eschew their passion temporarily, and place sport in proper perspective, in light of the cruel fate that had befallen their fellow human beings. One notable example was the postponement of the Ryder Cup golf matches scheduled to take place in England on September 28-30, 2001. This competition had taken place every two years since 1927 (except during World War II) between teams from Great Britain and the United States. There was little enthusiasm from players and fans for continuing the rivalry during this sombre climate. Consequently, the Ryder Cup matches were re-scheduled and took place a year later, in September 2002, at the same venue and with exactly the same teams.

Postponement of sporting events was always preferable to any thoughts of permanent cancellation. Political leaders of countries which had suffered from acts of terrorism, besides the United States, urged their citizens to resume as normal a life as possible. To do otherwise would mean a surrender of their freedom and represent a victory for the terrorists. After grieving, therefore, there was a widespread determination to resume the activities in the sporting calendar. Once leagues began to function again in various sports, tributes were paid to the victims of September 11. Black armbands were worn by many participants and respectful silences were observed in stadiums around the world. Within a few weeks, American and international sport appeared to be back to normal. But there were some inevitable and necessary permanent changes, particularly to do with security that would change the way of sport.

Sport certainly has not been immune to violent acts of political protests and/or terrorism prior to September 11, 2001. Indeed, sport's universal appeal and high profile make it vulnerable to those seeking a wide audience and publicity for their cause. The most notorious event occurred during a celebration of the world's largest multi-sport festival, the Summer Olympic Games, on September 5, 1972. On that date Arab terrorists assassinated eleven Israeli athletes and coaches in the Olympic Village. Five of the terrorists were subsequently killed, as well as one German policeman, in a shootout at the local airport. Despite the "Munich massacre" as it was called, the Games went on after a service of remembrance.

Sport Tourism in the New Millennium

Since 1972, the hosts of succeeding Olympic Games and other major sporting events have found it necessary to spend millions of dollars on security, within facilities said to resemble "armed fortresses" because of these precautions. And after September 11, such motivations have increased and security arrangements accelerated. The Super Dome in New Orleans was said to have resembled a military compound for Super Bowl XXXVI on February 3, 2002. Soldiers were employed on the ground and sharpshooters on the roof, and a no-fly zone for civilian aircraft was enforced above the stadium. Fans were urged to show up at least four hours before the game in order to get everyone through security before the start of the game. Similar arrangements were made for the two-week Winter Olympics held in Salt Lake City during February 2002, and were reported to exceed $300 million. Unfortunately such expense will remain the pattern for the future as security will be one of the largest budget items for major sporting events.

While such safeguards may be regrettable, and nostalgic feelings may persist for past times when such intrusions were absent, it is important to note that the masses by-and-large are now accepting them and adapting accordingly. Governments have acted to increase security at airports and borders, and travellers are now required to arrive much earlier to accommodate the stricter security procedures. That all these adjustments are being incorporated and tolerated is confirmed by the renewed enthusiastic attendance at major sports events. Clearly Sport Tourism is too much a part and parcel of every day life, too integral a component of society to be abandoned. The environment has been altered irrevocably, but signs are that Sport Tourism will fully recover its' status in human affairs in the near future. Supporting this optimistic forecast are predictions that the global economy is rebounding from its' recession, which is welcome news for the Sport Tourism industry.

Summary

Despite the hiatus caused by the tragedy of September 11, 2001, tourism will regain its' prestigious position in the world economy and sport will survive as the world's biggest social phenomenon. Their symbiotic relationship, manifested in Sport Tourism will continue to prosper as travel becomes safer and sports facilities are made even more secure. Shortly after "9/11", the Canadian Tourism Commission carried an article entitled "Sport tourism means good business". It indicated that "sport is a major industry and a significant travel motivator and sport travel is valued at $1.3 billion annually and growing" (*Communique*, December 2001,). There is no indication that the growth in Sport Tourism will slow down in the future.

References

Canadian Tourism Commission (2001), *Communique*, December, Volume 11, Issue 5.

8th IAAF World Athletics Championships, Edmonton, Alberta.
(S. Petersen Photograph)

6750001